New Typographic Design

New Typographic Design

Roger Fawcett-Tang

With an introduction and essays

by David Jury

Yale University Press

Published in North America by
Yale University Press
P.O. Box 209040
New Haven, CT 06520-9040
U.S.A.
www.yalebooks.com

First published in 2007 by
Laurence King Publishing Ltd, London

Library of Congress Control Number: 2006938720

ISBN: 978-0-300-11775-2

10 9 8 7 6 5 4 3 2

Designed by Struktur Design Limited
Picture research by Roger Fawcett-Tang
Photography by Roger Fawcett-Tang
Cover photography by Xavier Young
3D lettering supplied by www.vialetter.com

Printed in China

contents

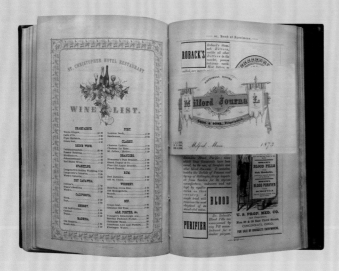

Fads, freaks and fancies (Part 1: Change is bad)

Less than 50 years after the first European book had been created using movable type, the printed word was established as the medium that could be trusted above all other – a remarkable feat, achieved through fine scholarship and breathtaking craftsmanship by pioneer printers such as Nicolas Jenson, Erhard Ratdolt and Aldus Manutius. Soon, however, entrepreneurs, attracted by the lure of the profits that printing could bring, moved in to publish cheap almanacs, cookbooks, pseudo-scientific treatises and the like. The idea that print might remain a purveyor purely of 'fine thoughts' was speedily undone.

During the next 300 years, the amount of printing steadily grew. Then, in the latter half of the 18th century, due to improved transport links and the influence of printed matter, a major cultural obsession with Roman antiquity swept across Europe with unprecedented speed. By 1800, every field of the arts appeared to be under the spell of Rome's *beau idéal* as all the major cities attempted to be the 'new Rome'. Appropriately, it was an Italian, Giambattista Bodoni, who captured the austere grandeur of neoclassicism in the printed word.

Bodoni's typefaces and, just as importantly, the way he designed his books with them, brought into question the entire nature and purpose of typography and the function of the printer/typographer. This was the first time that the appearance of type had been consciously designed to reflect transient 'taste' and, in so doing, placed aesthetic considerations before readability. It is interesting to note that in his own lifetime Bodoni was lauded not only as a great typographer and printer, but also as a great artist.

Not surprisingly, Bodoni, like his faces, was criticized by some for having a brashness that was unbecoming in a typographer and printer. It was felt that such behaviour went against the essentially neutral, self-effacing tradition of the trade. The modern typographer, as epitomized by Bodoni, was consciously creating a more audacious, and certainly more conspicuous, role for himself in the task of bringing the author's words to the reader.

Bodoni's work exerted a huge influence on the typefoundries which, during the exciting, expansive period of the early 1800s, recognized the development of a new and very different application for type. The growing influence of the Industrial Revolution was providing commercial and technological opportunities for businesses and other organizations, which in turn required for the first time printed material that could not only explain, but also actively promote their products, services or events.

Traditional printers' reluctance to embrace these changes was part moral, part commercial and part practical. While the scholarly abilities of the printer might vary, the deep-rooted tradition of the print trade and its affiliated organizations was to provide the reader with access to information succinctly, even imperceptibly. Now, a new kind of author, perhaps a soap manufacturer, shipping merchant or theatre impresario, was requesting that the printer not only present his words cleanly and without error, but also that the printer should present him as trustworthy, successful, wholesome and entertaining. Such requests, involving blatant persuasion or concealment, were considered by many printers as demeaning. Such requests certainly had little to do with the traditional ethics of printing and were something for which the print trade was ill prepared.[1]

To accommodate such requirements, the producer of this new kind of material, known as a job (or jobbing) printer, had to adapt his skills quickly to the design of posters, handbills, labels etc that incorporated qualities that attracted, surprised and impressed. In short, he had to be able to make type perform a role that was the exact opposite of its traditional mannered discretion.

The new and innovative typefaces designed specifically for this purpose were referred to as (among other names) novelties, freaks and fancies. Only if the type first caught the attention of the reader would its message be read: as such, there was a premium on novelty. The ability to make words as large as possible, or appear large by their boldness, or simply attract attention by their 'strangeness' of form, became key. As promotion grew ever more pervasive, so novelty had to become more pronounced.

It was in 1803 that Robert Thorne of the Fann Street Typefoundry in London produced the first typeface designed specifically for display (as opposed to textual) purposes. Thorne, and his successor at Fann Street, William Thorowgood, along with another English typefounder, Vincent Figgins, were the among the first great innovators of novelty types and produced, long before anyone else, Fat Faces and bold Egyptians that were 'unique in their boldness and deformity'.[2] The specimen books that these typefoundries produced during the first half

1 Of course, it is naive to imagine that the printer of a book was unaware of the potential of print to provide status and respect for the author. Every author would surely consider authority a prerequisite, and with the same aims in mind the author and/or publisher would seek to commission a printer whose bookwork, in design, materials, printing and binding, reflected the perceived standard. Authority, status, kudos came with being perceived as being part of the establishment, of upholding the status quo.

2 Talbot Baines Reed, quoted by John Lewis, *Printed Ephemera*, Faber and Faber, London, 1969.

of the 19th century are small in format but huge in their visual impact.

These raw and quite revolutionary typefaces were usually designed anonymously by employees of commercial foundries supplying commercial printers. Because their intentions were purely commercial, considerations of historical precedence or typographic principle had little influence upon their designs. The results might have been considered 'naive',[3] but they are also remarkable examples of intuitive craftsmanship unhindered by convention. The alternative view, and one certainly shared by those printers who remained in bookwork, however, was that this was a period in which 'the businessman defeated and annihilated the philosopher and poet'.[4]

Other typefoundries quickly began to produce their own ranges of display types, generally designed by taking 'normal' letterforms and accentuating particular characteristics to a grotesque level. Not to be outdone, another typefoundry would then take the most profitable of these 'grotesques' and accentuate its characteristics. 'Grotesque' or 'Grot' became a common description for bold types with no serifs and a relatively even thickness of line (providing a maximum printed area). Their simplicity of form meant that dramatically extended or condensed versions could be designed with relative ease. Egyptian types (so-called because of the fascination at the time for the archaeological discoveries along the Nile) had the same evenness and boldness of line but with huge, emphatic, slab serifs.

Demand stimulated technological innovation. The introduction of the combined pantograph and router in 1834 revolutionized type manufacture by allowing different sizes and styles of a font to be generated from a single drawing. Size was suddenly important, encouraging the substitution of metal for wood in the manufacture of types as posters and public notices became the most prevalent and popular form of communication on the street. This dramatic change in scale was another factor in altering printers' perceptions. Suddenly type was a more flexible medium, something that could be bought in compressed or expanded form, manufactured bolder or lighter, given outlines and drop shadows.

Since attraction was a prime motivator, the relationship between letters within a font became more important than the identity of the individual characters. In other words, legibility was not the prime concern any more: letters were being turned into images, something to be seen and recognized rather than 'read'. Typography had found a new purpose – in the pursuit of which, to be successful, all printers had to turn all previous rules (which, of course, related to textual typography) on their heads.

These new types were unrefined. They had no history, no lineage, no breeding.[5] Distinctive type was, by definition, considered by many in the book-print trade to be ugly. Change had been unnecessary and the results were therefore vulgar. In general, a book would be designed to look like every other book. The more typically 'bookish' its attributes, the better its design. The design of the type was instrumental in achieving this. But equally it was clear that, for advertising purposes, the fine, open-faced serifed book types, when forced into irregular-shaped boxes or squeezed between engraved images, were proving hopelessly inadequate. Despite this, there remained an influential number of printers – generally those with access (and/or the inclination to write articles) to the specialist print-trade press – who argued that the new types were bringing the printing profession into disrepute. Here is Dr Edmund Fry, a letter founder, writing

3 Nicolette Gray, *Nineteenth-Century Ornamented Types*, Faber and Faber, 1976.

4 John Lewis, *Printed Ephemera*, Faber and Faber, London, 1969.

5 'To be well designed a table, a pot or a chair must be well bred' (Lethaby). The juxtaposition of classic design and social class was a common phenomenon in Britain well into the latter part of the 20th century.

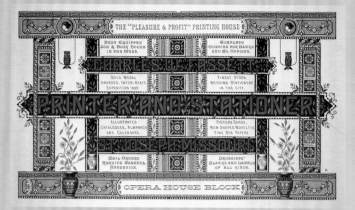

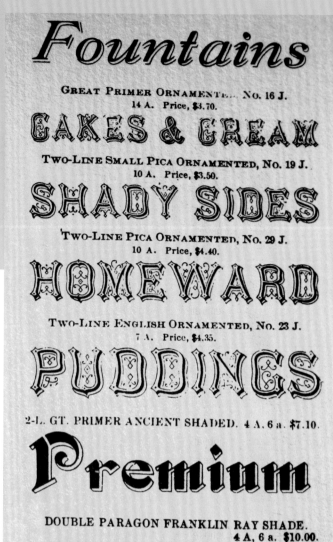

in 1828: 'a rude pernicious and most unclassical innovating system… the most injurious and dislocating ravages on the property of every Letter Founder and Printer in the Kingdom, by the introduction of Fancy letters, of various anomalous forms, with names as appropriate. Disgraceful is a profession once held so sacred as to have its operations confined to sacred buildings of the highest class.'[6]

Thorne, Thorowgood and Figgins clearly would not have shared this point of view, nor, in North America, the Wells family in their Cincinnati typefoundry and many others. Initially, typefoundries in North America made blatant copies of the successful imported British display types, but by the middle of the 19th century, with an unrestrained and now burgeoning advertising industry of their own to feed, the full potential of display face design was being explored. New display types flowed onto the market; hundreds of different varieties of letters that are impossible to describe, let alone classify. The work of the jobbing printer showed splendid appreciation of this new typographic material and invention in its application, whether for starkly simple public notices, highly complex playbills, or delicate labels for tea, biscuits and tobacco.

Suddenly, the printer had a multitude of options, not just in the number of typefaces available but in the way they might be used. Suddenly the old rules no longer applied. But, needless to say, nothing in the traditional training of a printer prepared him for this. Typography for bookwork remained the bedrock of the printer's training despite the new opportunities available in commercial printing. Resistance to change was, to a large degree, due to the fact that most of an apprentice's training involved working alongside the 'old hands' whose attitudes were not, generally, conducive to independent thinking. Printshops, while vigorously hierarchical, were also interdisciplinary in structure, and a young apprentice would not be encouraged to adopt any methods with which everyone else was not already familiar. Unlike today, 'youth' had no status whatsoever in the 19th century.

While genuinely new fonts designed for a new purpose heralded a potential fresh start for those printers willing to try their hand at something different, for the print 'establishment' the only imperative was that the traditional typographic knowledge and skills of bookwork must not be tainted by newness. To achieve this, it was clearly considered insufficient just to praise the finer points of textual setting.

6 This resistance to change within sections of the printing industry would persist. This is from Sayers and Stuart, *Art and Practice of Printing*, Pitman, Vol. 1, 1932, a seven-volume manual for students: 'With regard to some freakish typefaces now in use, little need be said… Novelty there must be in these restless times but illegibility and ugly types, popular as they must be for a time, soon pass away.'

Instead, every opportunity had to be taken to denigrate the 'antics' of the jobbing printer through the columns of the various printers' magazines of the day. These attacks were relentless and savage. When William Morris set up his Kelmscott Press in 1896, he was seen as both a saviour and a beacon: at last a return to basics and the sanity of formal standards.

The opportunity for change had been refused: the printing industry would modernize technically but intellectually it would never come to terms with the notion that typography and its arrangement could or should be 'meddled with'. Consequently, the growing advertising industry was forced to look elsewhere or devise its own means of achieving the innovative typography it required.

The roots of graphic design are often described as being in the 'admirable' work of pioneering independent book typographers such as William Pickering (Britain) and Bruce Rogers (USA). However, the true roots (certainly the true spirit) of graphic design are surely in the truly innovative and truly despised work of the 19th-century jobbing printer, who was able to embrace the fearful notion of the unpredictable and the ever-changing nature of commercial demand.

(far left) Another specimen page from *Ye American Printer's Specimen Exchange* (1886), but very different in both composition and use of colour. Images of neoclassicism and medievalism mixed with typefaces associated with the 'wild west'. The main letters are printed gold.

(left) Detail from a page of *Fancy Types* (Cincinnati Type Foundry Catalog, 1877). The terms 'English', 'Gt Primer' and 'Double Paragon' are descriptions of size. These are medieval or 'Artistic' styles, rather than the heavy industrial styles of font with which we have come to associate 19th-century North America.

(right) Hans Leistikow poster for Futura which was designed by Paul Renner for the German Bauer Type Foundry in 1927.

Fads, freaks and fancies (Part 2: Change is good)

The innovative typographer is almost always a young typographer. Today, not only is it accepted that we need innovative typography but also that it is, on the whole, a 'good thing'. This notion is supported even when creative endeavour requires (as it almost always does) that the typographer display contempt for the typographic establishment. This is also celebrated as being a 'good thing', because, of course, the typographic establishment is generally composed of typographers who once aspired to be innovative.

Innocence enables conviction to overrule convention, ensuring that the 'right' solution is pursued regardless of social and political sensibilities or, indeed, financial implications. Profit is often of little interest in these early, less complicated years. But this state of mind cannot be maintained indefinitely and, after 20 years of age, it is surely impossible for anyone to remain entirely innocent. Students are often told by their tutors (in a rather apologetic way, I have always thought) that they are being taught the conventions so that they can better understand what they are *not* doing.[7] The ethos of the art school (which is where typographers are now taught) is that students are encouraged to create change, 'make a difference' and be noticed. Despite this, how often do we hear the latest typographer to be placed on a pedestal describing his or her student days in the following terms: 'I had to fight my tutors every inch of the way. They tried to hold me back but I refused to be beaten.' Another typographic hero (ho-hum).

It seems that no worse fate can befall a typography student than to be described as being 'like everyone else' because being 'like everyone else' is a category that, in their mind, comprises the mediocre. Convention means predictable; means boring; means irrelevant. Whereas newness means (or at least is intended to be) unpredictable, surprising, in fact the elixir of life.

The young typographic warriors being referred to here are, in fact, usually graphic design students, although the printing fraternity preferred to call them 'art students', as if to distance itself from the antics of the 'flashy little stylists' (as Beatrice Warde described them in 1954).[8] And yet, in 1954, while graphic design in Britain was establishing a distinctive role for itself through the divergent work of (for example) Abram Games, Tom Eckersley and F.H.K. Henrion (and in North America, Paul Rand, Alexey Brodovitch, Reid Miles et al), it was,

in educational terms, still very much in its infancy and being taught with severe self-imposed constraints. During the 20th century, graphic design, as we understand the term today, developed considerably more slowly in Britain than in mainland Europe or North America. The reasons for this provide a direct connection to the treatment by the printing 'elite' of the jobbing printer – essentially, the earliest incarnation of the graphic designer – in the 19th century.

One of the first, specific graphic design courses in Britain was set up in 1949 at the Royal College of Art, but its content remained determinedly book-oriented, refusing to pay anything more than lip service to the growing international fields of graphic communication and advertising. The typographic establishment in Britain remained enmeshed with those aspects of printed matter that could be considered as 'worthy' (books, again) because historic, aesthetic and technical precedence could be found there.

Those early Royal College tutors were simply maintaining the status quo. Some 45 years earlier, W.R. Lethaby, principal of the RCA, had said: 'A perfect chair or table or book has to be very well bred.'[9] Values of heritage, tradition and status were often described in terms of class and breeding, a trait that would persist until at least the middle of the 20th century. And it is tempting to suggest that the perceived value of timeless or 'classic' design – generally described as being the result of a process of refinement independent of the whims of fashion – was also linked to the notion of social or 'class' status. One of those early RCA tutors, John Lewis, drew a clear distinction between the printer of books (the classic formula) and the printer of everything else (make it up as you go along) in his book *Printed Ephemera*: 'The printer of books tended to be a sophisticated tradesman, if not a scholar; the jobbing printer and the trade engraver were often as not barely literate. In producing their tobacco wrappers, broadsheets and chapbooks, they were practising what amounted to a peasant art.'[10]

7 As Steven Heller (self-confessed student drop-out and self-taught designer) explains, 'a really good undergraduate education packs the student's brain with so many damn rules (and infuriating opinions) that rule-breaking is inevitable.' *Eye* 56, 2005, p. 74.

8 Beatrice Warde, 'The Pencil Draws a Vicious Circle', *The Crystal Goblet*, The Sylvan Press, 1955.

9 Sylvia Backemeyer and Theresa Gronberg, *W.R. Lethaby: Architect, Design and Education*, Lund Humphries, London, 1984.

10 John Lewis, *Printed Ephemera*, Faber and Faber, London, 1969.

For Lewis, a method of working that required an emotive response was ill-disciplined and crude. The results may be worthy of study (Lewis's book is full of praise for the ingenuity of the jobbing printer) but the nature of that ingenuity is generally discussed in terms of an innocent – a child – at play. Clearly (in Britain at least) the overriding opinion in design education was that design must maintain the values of the past, both cultural and aesthetic, making it impervious to external change. Change had not yet become a prerogative of design.

In Weimar, some 30 years earlier, the Bauhaus had taken the opposite stance to virtually everything that represented the previous order. Its initial ideology was gleaned, for the most part, from the cultural and social concerns of William Morris, whose benign British socialism drew a parallel between working methods and conditions, and the quality of the chair, table or book being 'manufactured'. The Bauhaus, however, took the worker out of the equation and, instead, turned its attention wholly to the aesthetics of mechanization and mass production. While the Bauhaus responded enthusiastically to the vitality and energy of the American city and revered its skyscraper architecture, it showed a total lack of enthusiasm for traditional German literary, visual and craft culture. This was both alarming and quite unacceptable to the Nazi regime which, by closing the school down, inadvertently gave the Bauhaus, and the modernism it expounded (ornament is crime; less is more; form follows function), mythical status.

By the mid-1930s, North America and, more specifically, New York had become the proverbial melting pot of European immigrants. Here, commercial art was an established subject, even taught at secondary school,[11] and it was a profession well suited, it seems, to immigrant children, raised during the Great Depression but who had developed a passion for American popular culture. Being outsiders, they took nothing for granted and devoured comics, television and cinema with relish. Many also dabbled in jazz and other popular music forms.

The Bauhaus and its fate had been followed closely in North America, where, not surprisingly, there was a great deal of sympathy for its ideals. Many of the New York graduates would continue their education at art schools such as the Pratt Institute, Parsons School of Design, the Art Students League and the Cooper Union and take courses in poster design, illustration, advertising and typography that

11 Steven Heller, 'When Art Directors Walked the Earth: New York in the Fifties and Sixties', *TypoGraphic* 65, 2006.

12 Ibid.

combined Bauhausian methodology with mass advertising and publishing techniques at secondary-school level.[12] The role models for these students were not those American supporters of William Morris, who established the so-called 'Colonial Revival', those self-styled representatives of 'high culture' (the status quo) such as D.B. Updike, Will Bradley, Bruce Rogers, and Frederic Goudy (whose first typeface was called Camelot). Instead they turned to bold, innovative, European poster designers such as Lucian Bernhard, A.M. Cassandre, and E. McKnight Kauffer. This generation of young designers was ambitious for change, relished the brash competitiveness of print for mass communication (previously considered 'low culture') and gave it a modernism that lifted, embraced and, indeed, extended American iconography by its novel use of type and photographic imagery.

The lack of interest in Britain for modernism was due in no small part to a general suspicion of anything emanating from Germany during the 1930s. The association of mechanization and the aesthetic of the machine with the build-up of German armaments might seem crude now but the connection must have felt very real at the time. As far as British typography was concerned, its voice was largely provided by Stanley Morison, typographic advisor at the Monotype Corporation (and, later, typographic advisor to *The Times*), who argued for the inviolability of such governing typographic values as convention, reason and comprehension. His famous essay *First Principles of Typography* is notable for its lack of comment concerning the work of the modernists in Germany. Morison believed that the investigations undertaken by the Bauhaus typographers had nothing to do with (far left) Poster designed by E. McKnight Kauffer in 1934 for an oil company. Kauffer was able to reduce the complexity of Constructivism to simple, instantly iconic forms, a feat greatly admired by the burgeoning contemporary North American design profession.

(left) The magazine *Advertising Arts* promoted creative art direction, leading the way for the post-war revolution. This 1934 cover by John Atherton (New York), illustrating the modern designer, combines the unlikely influences of Russian Constructivism and Dada to promote advertising to American commerce.

(right) *Ark*, the magazine of the Royal College of Art, London. Designed by Melvyn Gill, 1963.

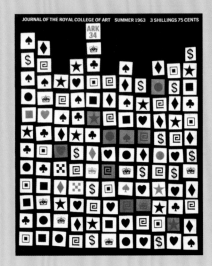

typography because (he thought) they were making art out of something that he considered to be a service.[13]

By the mid-1950s it was clear that a visual mass-media revolution was under way, and very clearly it was not happening in Britain! Indeed, it was not until the late 1950s that Britain, now fully recovered from its post-war trauma, discovered the possibilities of consumerism through the power of television and cinema. American programmes and films bedazzled British audiences with images of 'American plenty': huge fridges full of pre-packed food; joyful 'casual' clothes; supermarket plazas; brightly coloured cars iced in chrome. A few years later, Britain's own media revolution took off and the culture of change was embraced.

The abandonment of restraints and a receptivity to continual change are fundamental characteristics of the times in which we live. They have been proved to be good for business and, finally, they are good for the sensory and intellectual quality of our lives. Of course, without restraints, horrible mistakes can be made and, undoubtedly, 'standards' have become woolly, to say the least. But how could it be otherwise? Flying in the face of convention, skirting the edge of social propriety,[14] provides diversity in all things and is a part of the spirit of any emerging technology and, naturally, the technology-makers are in the business of ensuring that change is relentless, desirable and generally 'good'.

Of course, not everyone is in thrall to change. Nor is the link between value and class entirely dead. Cultural diversity ensures this. Just a few years ago, a politician, criticizing an opponent for his lack of cultural perspicacity, described him as 'the kind of person who buys his own furniture'. This remark (putting aside its 'classic' mix of vicious snobbery and withering wit) reflects a disdain for newness and, more importantly, a reverence for objects that are designed and made to last (and, therefore, are able to be passed down from generation to generation). It is also important to say here that such deeply ingrained social attitudes were one of the key reasons for modernism being embraced so much more quickly and effectively in Europe and the USA than in Britain.

Nevertheless, while 'old' may sometimes be plainly superior, the genuinely 'new' always excites. 'Dependable and trusted' remains highly valued, but referring to past models can also be interpreted as a non-solution, a means of avoiding the problem, while

genuine newness – innovation – is not just participation, it is an act of leadership and the clearest sign of continued relevance. Indeed, such is the allure of newness that it is more common than not for something old and better to be replaced without question by something new and worse. But to make such a claim is to proclaim oneself irrelevant. It is often said that shopping is a way of restating one's relevance: 'I shop therefore I am!'

Today, change is taken for granted. It happens constantly. Change is the driving force behind both commercial and public institutions because it is, though often inappropriate, the easiest way for a management to demonstrate that it is 'managing'.

The design profession has benefited from such strategies because every time something needs changing, something needs designing. Designers have learned that being closer to corporate management means being closer to power and that this power provides status. Change has become power. But, of course, if change is carried out for the wrong reasons the designer will be seen as the instigator of what might be inappropriate, even irresponsible actions, and the resulting design perceived as mere camouflage to conceal or distract. However, we must be realistic (this is the real world, after all) and so, when a multinational company with, inevitably, a multinational problem asks for concealment, how many designers can afford to say no?

The inevitability of change suggests that typographic practice consists of the pursuit of an ever-swinging pendulum.[15] But it is far too depressing to imagine that the work of the responsible typographer is based on little more than a reaction against the work of the preceding generation. And even if there is an element of truth in this, with experience a typographer can develop convictions of more substance which need not lead to resistance or indifference to change. The process of design requires an inquiring and generous attitude and the opportunity to experiment and manoeuvre. But being relevant (modern?) should not require that a designer blindly follow the requisite style. 'Relevant' simply means being true to the time in which you live, true to the tools and the media with which you work, and truthful to the people with whom you are communicating. When this is possible, there is every reason to suppose that typography will continue to disrupt the rhythm of the pendulum. The work included in this book provides ample evidence of that.

13 Stanley Morison, *First Principles of Typography*, 2nd edn, Cambridge University Press, 1967. Also, Herbert Bayer (tutor at the Bauhaus) stated that, for typography at least, 'knowing nothing gave the Bauhaus tutors freedom to invent'.

14 Michael Rock, 'Fabien Baron, or Sex and a Singular Art Director', *I.D.*, May/June 1993.

15 Keith Robinson, 'Starting from Zero', *Emigre* 19, 1991

type as form

Working with conventional, commercially available typefaces focuses the designer's attention on the essential qualities of the font, paradoxically often resulting in designs that seek out new typographic directions. The clean typographic forms are sometimes adopted as the foundations on which the overall design is built.

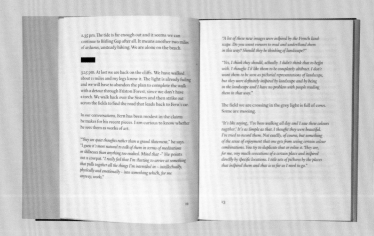

The pleasure of silence

The form typography takes dictates its volume. Of all the volume settings, 'mute' is the most difficult to achieve.

The 20th-century composer John Cage famously wanted to know what it felt like to experience true silence and so arranged to be placed in an anechoic (soundproof) chamber at Harvard University. After a period of adjustment, he realized he could still hear two sounds, one high and one low. Later, when he described these to the engineer he was told that the high one was his nervous system and the low one was his blood in circulation. Clearly, complete silence does not exist.[1]

The form that type is given and the form in which it is arranged determines and defines its function. There are many different methods of reading to suit a variety of purposes. We read to gain information through research and study, and we read to relax and be entertained. Directories and dictionaries are obviously designed to be used differently from newspapers, which, in turn, are different from novels. Typographic form follows function.

Reading is an insular, private, silent affair. Even in a room full of people (for example, the reading room of a public library) each person will be engrossed in their own thoughts. Even if the surroundings are noisy and boisterous (for example, a café or bar) a reader can consciously ignore these potentially disruptive activities and, effectively, make them evaporate.

Just as the reader can control extraneous noise, so the printed letters on the page can be made to evaporate as the reader forms images in his or her mind from the author's words. The typographer cannot control the noise that might surround the reader, but by careful arrangement of form and detailed adjustment he or she can contribute greatly to the essential ability of the printed word to evaporate for the reader. Appropriately, type and/or typography which refuses to evaporate in this way is often referred to as 'noise'.[2]

It is often said that to enable this vanishing trick to be accomplished, typography and typeface must be so 'normal' that the reader is never caused to look at the words or their arrangement. Nothing unusual, nothing to attract unwarranted attention to its individual form or to the way it is arranged. The result is that the reader can read without faltering. This is the selfless, entirely anonymous notion of 'service' described by Stanley Morison (page 10 of this book) that is provided by the typographer to both author and reader. This is, undoubtedly, a noble principle and one that attracts some graphic designers to specialize in typography.

In order to achieve silent typography it is generally assumed that all the typographer must do is to stick rigidly to the conventions. Such conventions, however, are anything but rigid, in fact they are often little more than a set of intentionally vague opinions.

Such opinions can be read in numerous books, Morison's *First Principles of Typography* being probably the best-known example.[3] But for a description of clear-cut typographic conventions there can be nothing better than the guides or manuals published by the larger printing houses during the 20th century.

These house style guides are generally aimed at a wider readership, including authors, editors, proofreaders and compositors, and address all aspects of typographic form as well as, for example, issues concerning spelling and punctuation. *Hart's Rules for Compositors and Readers* comes under this heading, its original title being *Hart's Rules for Compositors and Readers Employed at the Clarendon Press, Oxford* (1893).[4] Books such as this prescribed the company rules for those areas of typographic form and English usage where solutions to grammatical or technical problems might vary. The aim of house style guides was to standardize the process of typographic composition (its setting) and make it more efficient. The standardization of the text in this way also ensured a noiseless text for the reader.

The titles of such manuals suggest a conformity to prevailing standards: for example, DeVinne's *Correct Composition* (1901).[5] In fact, what these 'authorities' aimed to achieve was often less prescriptive than might be imagined. John Smith, in his *The Printer's Grammar* of 1755, aimed to provide 'conformity to a standard that the consensus of opinion recognises as good'. DeVinne's stated intention was 'to define the fixed practice of the greater number of authors and printers'.

What Smith, DeVinne and Hart recognized was that there are many aspects of good typography that are the result of the typographer's tacit knowledge of typographic form, a kind of sensory discernment that comes from a practical understanding of the raw materials and the vagaries thereof. The deference so often signalled in classic manuals to the compositor consistently acknowledges this fact.

abcdefghijklmnopqrstuvwxyz
ABCDEFGHIJKLMNOPQRSTUVWXYZ
ABCDEFGHIJKLMNOPQRSTUVWXYZ
0123456789 0123456789

Such deference exists because typographic conventions of a technical nature will always require ingenuity in their application, which, in turn, requires that the typographer maintain the motivation to interpret such rules. The following statement is from the first edition of *The Chicago Manual of Style* of 1906 and has been reprinted in every edition since. 'Rules and regulations… must be applied with a certain amount of elasticity. Exceptions will constantly occur, and ample room is left for individual initiative and discretion. [Rules and regulations] point the way and survey the road rather than remove the obstacles.'

The titles of these manuals suggest an ominously difficult read and, at first glance, everything about them (in their original typographic form) is designed to make them appear authoritative. And yet, once the reader has engaged with the texts, especially those of DeVinne and Hart, they are, perhaps surprisingly, very accessible and even humorous, and although undoubtedly authoritative, not nearly as authoritarian as might initially be expected.

There is an important point here. There is more to be seen on the printed page than a mere sequence of letters and that text communicates to the reader before a single word has been read. In fact, it is the qualities that distinguish the form of a document from a simple accumulation of letters that might, finally, be described as 'typography'. That we interpret the intentions of the author of a text before it is read is unavoidable and to ensure an 'effective' (intended) interpretation is a key function of the typographer.

Even the typeface itself (clearly a key decision, but no more important than the choice of size or weight, or how it is arranged) provides unavoidable signals. It is remarkable how much 'character' can be designed into a typeface which, later, can evaporate when the reader begins to read. The type designer Gerard Unger describes it like this: 'Only the basic shapes need to comply with what we are used to. To this conventional frame, the type designer applies the features that supply typefaces with their characteristics. Every designer has particular habits that ooze through in the typeface design.'[6]

There have been several attempts to design a 'universal' typeface with a sufficient range of weights and widths to make it fit all possible purposes. But every typeface is (or, more accurately, becomes) the product of its designer, of its time and place, and of its technology. These are characteristics which must, inevitably, add something to what the author wishes to communicate.

But it is also possible for a typeface to be the product of its author. A2/SW/HK design a different typeface for every client (above left), enabling them to produce letterforms that make direct reference in their details to a particular aspect of each different project. There is something vaguely anarchic about A2's celebrated lack of restraint which suggests a healthy lack of preciousness. Even in this digital age, their achievement is remarkable, and very flattering for the client.

Fonts that have established associations will, inevitably, contribute these to the sense of the author's words. The book *Morocco* (designed and produced by David Jury, above) consists of two texts set in two columns, side by side. Monotype Grot (unjustified) is used to present an often uncouth, uncensored text, in contrast with Monotype Baskerville (justified) which is used for its English, stiff, upright stance and presents the self-censored version intended for publication. The arrangement of the texts allows readers to see what the author thought (in 1934) but the sensor would not allow them to read.

A text in which a reader is subsumed by the thoughts of the author is one that succeeds in connecting with the habits and expectations of its audience. This does not, however, mean the type or the typography is somehow 'neutral'. As discussed above, neutral type does not exist. It should also be remembered that the purpose of generating text is never for it to remain unread. Printed matter must be designed into something, an object that can attract the attention of those whose attention is sought. In other words, it must solicit. But the means of attraction must not sacrifice the message. The typographer aims to create typographic forms that both attract the reader while enhancing the meaning of the author's words. This is a precarious balancing act, but when it succeeds – and there are numerous successful examples on the following pages – typographic communication is not only fluent, but also inviting and exciting.

Typography invites rational thought, and controlled and directed communication. Consciously or unconsciously, it creates and preserves social links, and provides a remarkable parallel to social form and function.

1 John Cage, *Silence*, Calder and Boyars, London, 1968.

2 Shannon and Weaver, *The Mathematical Theory of Communication*, 1949.

3 Stanley Morison, *First Principles of Typography*, 2nd edn, Cambridge University Press, 1967.

4 Horace Hart, *Rules for Compositors and Readers*, Oxford University Press, 1904 (and numerous reprintings since).

5 Theodore Low DeVinne, *Correct Composition*, The Century Company, New York, 1901.

6 Gerard Unger, 'Legible?' in Michael Bierut, William Drenttel, Steven Heller and D.K. Holland, *Looking Closer*, Allsworth Publishers, USA, 1994.

Design	Saturday
Project	J. Lindeberg Denim
Category	Visual identity
Date	2005

In a kind of act of self-censorship, the identity features a series of blocks of solid black printed where the typography should be. A strong distinctive style is established by keeping all printed material in black and white, with the type reversed out of panels to create graphic building blocks. This theme is continued in-store, with the brand's shops using the same jagged blocks for display tables and shelves.

Design	Studio Philippe Apeloig
Project	Year of Brazil in France
Category	Poster
Date	2005

This purely typographic poster produced to promote the 'Year of Brazil in France' festival uses the Brazilian flag colours of gold, green and blue. Unlike much of the output from Apeloig, who designs unconventional bespoke fonts, this poster uses a clean, bold, slightly condensed sans serif. Some of the letterforms are reversed out of blocks of colour while others are butted up to each other, creating a great typographic energy.

Design	Saturday
Project	Florence
Category	Visual identity
Date	2005

This clean typographic identity for a London-based art agent/gallery uses Helvetica as its main driving force. Elements of type are either underlined or reversed out of blocks of colour in a bitmap fashion. The strong simple colour palette helps to reinforce the brand.

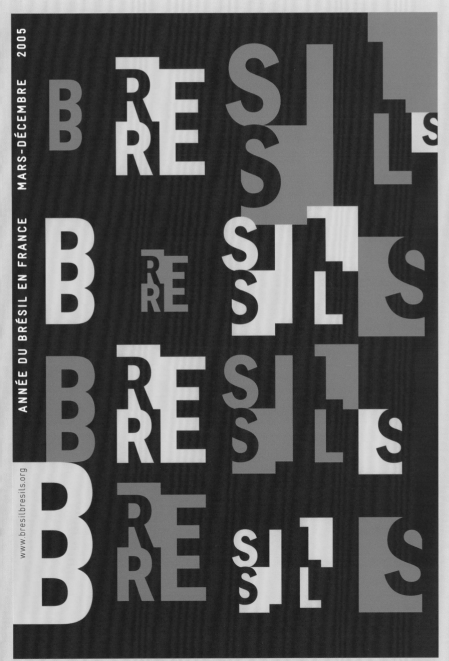

Design	Sans + Baum
Project	26 Letters
Category	Poster
Date	2004

Twenty-six ISTD members were each paired with a writer from the writers' professional body 26. The brief was to write and design a poster using a letter of the alphabet as a starting point. Given the letter 'e', writer Tom Lynham suggested producing a periodic table of the emotions and came up with a set of words from which the designer made a final selection, using the grid structure of the original table as a basis for the design.

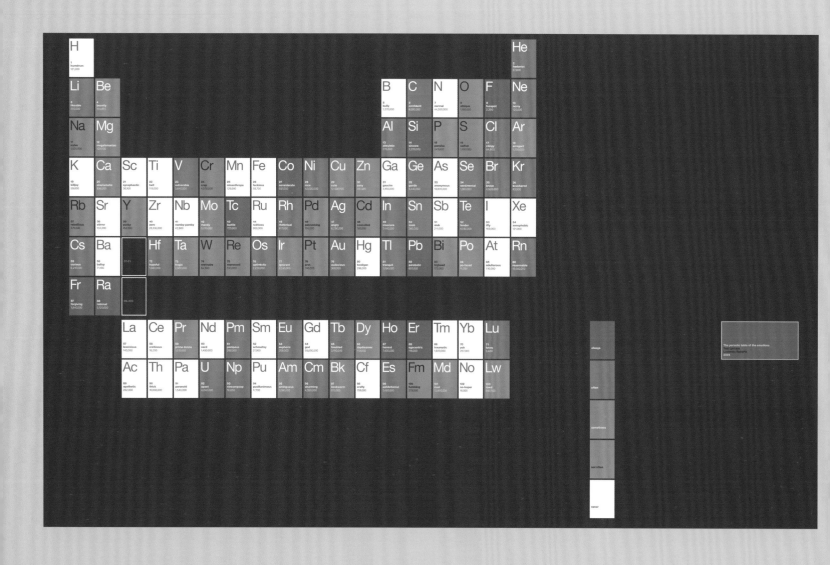

Design	Sans + Baum
Project	TypoGraphic 59
Category	ISTD journal
Date	2002

Every issue of *TypoGraphic* is created by a different designer. For this issue the designer wanted the first impression to be of typography and nothing else, so all the images were contained within perforated Chinese-bound pages. Helvetica is used throughout in just one point size. Owing to the clever imposition of the pages, the designer was able to print sections using a series of special strong colours and maintain four-colour sections for the illustrations. The use of strong blocks and panels of typography helps to emphasize the grid system.

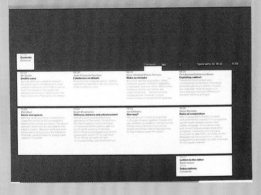

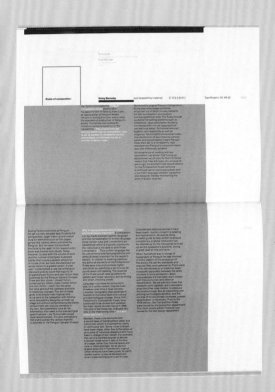

Design	Helmut Schmid
Project	'86 04 26: When the Birds Fly Again
Category	Poster
Date	1994

Two versions of this poster were produced, printed in blue and black (shown here) and red and black. The posters were created to commemorate the nuclear disaster at Chernobyl. The delicacy of the typographic proportions and placement is offset by the out-of-register colour printing, which creates a sense of disturbance in the midst of typographic harmony.

Design	Helmut Schmid
Project	Design Is Attitude
Category	Poster
Date	1998

Collaging together poetry by T.S. Eliot and correspondence between the Swiss designer Hans-Rudolf Lutz and Helmut Schmid, this poster combines heterogeneous elements but manages to maintain a sense of order at the same time. Printed in dark blue, hierarchy is created out of the different densities of type, from the light handwritten timetable to the letter from Schmid to Lutz set in large Univers and the small typewritten letter from Lutz to Schmid. These different elements are held together by the thick solid block on the left edge and the series of vertical rules.

when the birds
fly again

when the people
laugh again

when the plants
grow again

when the flowers
bloom again

when the fishes
swim again

then let Chernobyl be our reminder
then let Chernobyl be our lesson

'86 04 26

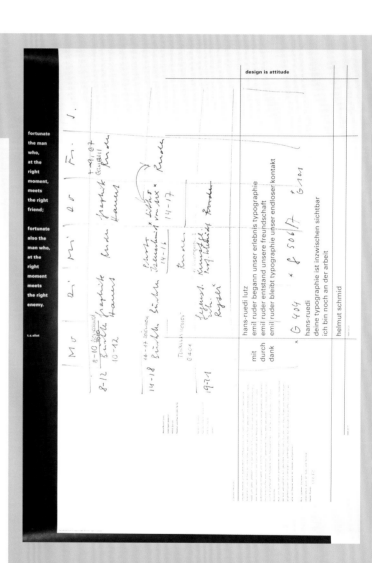

Design	Helmut Schmid
Project	On Typography
Category	Poster
Date	2000

Created for a talk given by Schmid at Kobe Design University in Japan, this poster was produced in a bilingual English/Japanese design which is beautifully clean and pure, and simply printed in black on a white stock. The four columns used at the top of the poster for text information are also employed for the positioning of the title, with the word 'typography' split into three parts. This allows for the letterforms to be printed large and so maximize the impact of the pure lines of Univers, the chosen font.

Design	Non-Format
Project	The Wire: Issue 250
Category	Magazine design
Date	2004

The pure simple brilliance of this cover for the contemporary music magazine is achieved by just working with the standard typographic elements of the masthead and step-and-repeating them off the page. The result is a stocastic pattern of fragments of type, which sums up the issue's lead feature, 'In Praise of the Riff'. The cover stands out on the crowded newsstand by emptying itself of all standard features, even (almost) the masthead. Proof that anarchy can be born of purity.

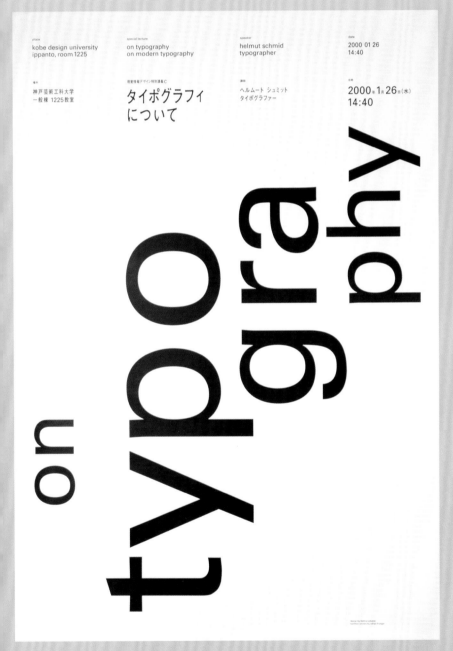

Design	Mode
Project	DaMa Font
Category	Typeface design
Date	2006

Beginning life as an identity for the typefoundry Dalton Maag, the DaMa logo has been extended into a full typeface. The fat rounded letterforms have a retro quality which is brought up to date by the reduced, minimal shape of each character. The font is only available in one heavy weight, which is generated in both a solid and an outline variant.

Design	Mode
Project	Dalton Maag: Practice Journal 2004
Category	Brochure
Date	2004

Produced for a typefoundry, this brochure highlights a series of bespoke corporate fonts created by it. Large fragments of the fonts are shown against photographic backdrops relevant to each case study. The typography is interwoven with screen grabs of the fonts under construction.

Design	Mode
Project	Synopsis
Category	Visual identity / printed material
Date	2005

Formed as a sub-brand to Dalton Maag, Synopsis uses the same DaMa font. However, the hard round edges of the letters are softened through the use of graduated coloured tints, the radiated colour from each letterform overlapping with the next to create a rich translucent effect. A white keyline is used to emphasize the true edge of each character. A promotional brochure was produced to launch the new brand. This builds up the letterforms progressively over the pages, with the full logo only being revealed at the end.

Design	Struktur Design
Project	24-Hour Clock
Category	Poster
Date	2003

This self-initiated poster project typographically illustrates the numerical contents of a 24-hour period of time. A sequence of small numbers in ten-second intervals forms the framework on which the minutes and hours are positioned. The result is a piece of typography in which the natural rivers running through the numbers form a random pattern that fluctuates throughout the course of the day.

Design	Struktur Design
Project	Minutes
Category	Diary
Date	2002

The concertina-folded pages of this diary extend to almost 3m (10ft) in length. The year is broken down into its constituent minutes, all 525,060 of them, which are printed in fluorescent pink continuously over the pages, with the days, weeks and months overprinted in warm grey and black. Similar to the '24-Hour Clock' poster project (left), the rhythmic nature of the numerical sequence plays a key part in the appearance of the work.

Design	Exposure
Project	Self-Portrait
Category	Poster
Date	2005

This poster, produced in a self-published run of 150 copies, features six columns of iTunes folders. It comments on the changing face of the record collection and explores ideas of identity through music. Typographically it relies on the words and default screen type to convey its message.

Design	Exposure
Project	Midnight in a Perfect World
Category	Poster
Date	2005

A self-published run of 600 posters was created as a New Year's greetings card. The design features a long list of things not to do in the new year, printed in red and set in bold Neue Helvetica. The list ranges from the sensible to the light-hearted and humorous.

Don't drink as much as last year. Don't smoke as much as last year. Don't rule out not smoking at all. Don't smoke the whole cigarette. Don't drink beer at home. Don't run with scissors. Don't rule out putting the cork back in a wine bottle. Don't eat cheese everyday. Don't spill your drink. Don't spill other people's drinks. Don't buy enormous rounds of drinks for people you don't know. Don't be frugal. Don't talk about dieting at the dinner table. Don't eat bread. Don't drink in bars that don't have a pre-defined closing time. Don't be afraid to dance in bars and clubs where no-one else is dancing. Don't be afraid of dancing spontaneously in environments that are not normally used for dancing. Don't dance in a style that is mocking someone else. Don't stop till you get enough. Don't drink sugary sodas. Don't substitute water with sugar free sodas. Don't eat as much red meat. Don't forego opportunities to ingest more vegetables. Don't be close minded towards the potential benefits of vegetarianism. Don't forget that there are lots of valid reasons to become a vegetarian over and above the love of animals. Don't get mercury poisoning from tuna or swordfish. Don't drink coffee after midday. Don't eat huge amounts of steak and eggs after prescribing to the latest dietary fad. Don't stop exercising once January has passed. Don't bite your nails. Don't chew the bits that you bite off your nails. Don't pick the skin around your nails. Don't forget to floss and rinse with a fluoride based mouthwash at least twice a day. Don't be afraid of the dentist. Don't eat fried food during the week unless its a holiday or a special occasion such as a birthday or a friends birthday. Don't leave clothes in the washer so they go musty. Don't wear clothes just once unless you wear them out on a big night out or exercise in them. Don't buy new clothes that are exactly the same as the clothes you bought six months ago. Don't buy clothes that are exactly the same as the clothes you bought six years ago. Don't be intimidated by bright colors. Don't listen to a word anyone says about your look. Don't read too much into what the media are reporting to be this seasons new look. Don't hesitate to change your look if four or more people in your local bar look almost exactly like you. Don't overdo the color coordination thing. Don't wear collars with sneakers unless they are Converse. Don't underestimate the importance of the lacing patterns in your sneakers. Don't buy things on credit except in emergencies. Don't buy vinyl that you already have as an mp3 unless you are sure that you will play it out at a party. Don't buy music through the iTunes music store unless you are sure you will not ever have the urge to play it at party. Don't duplicate formats. Don't overuse words such as basically, totally, like, exactly, whatever to the detriment of a more expressive vocabulary. Don't say oh my god. Don't say dude. Don't say rad. Don't take up hobbies that you are not interested in because you like the idea of them. Don't recommend things to other people that you have yet to experience yourself. Don't stop going to the movies. Don't keep anything that is scratched. Don't worry about what you eat whilst at the movies as you are partaking in a form of escapism that transcends the boundaries of the screen. Don't get upset that everyone is into apple now and there aren't that many windows users left to argue with. Don't be scared of change. Don't cast aspersions against entire nations based on the actions of their leadership. Don't use religion as an excuse for violence. Don't form opinions on foreign countries and ideologies based on information that you have received from your native media. Don't generalize. Don't be so politically correct. Don't feel you have to avoid harmless stereotypes that have been formed through thousands of years of observation. Don't stop exploring. Don't stop visiting a country through fear of violence unless there is a good chance you will be shot on arrival at the airport. Don't cry for me Argentina. Don't play back to spinners in June. Don't stop believing that you will avoid relegation. Don't be ashamed of being proud of your country of origin. Don't totally close yourself off to contemporary music because you are too busy unearthing the myriad gems of the past. Don't get aggressive with people who say they don't really like music. Don't bad mouth people who leave the country just because you'd like to do the same but have never got around to it. Don't move to a new country and start hating the country you left just to try and make yourself feel you don't miss it dearly. Don't adopt new regional accents and colloquialisms immediately. Don't stay up late during the week. Don't wear odd socks. Don't pick your nose in public. Don't pick your nose and eat it. Don't pick your nose and roll it up into a ball. Don't forget that cars have windows and that people can see into them. Don't think that not having car or health insurance makes you somehow bohemian. Don't run over pedestrians. Don't get hit by a car when crossing the road. Don't Jaywalk. Don't talk on the phone when driving. Don't smoke in the car whilst talking on the phone whilst driving. Don't be so vain about bicycle helmets. Don't ride a bike at night without lights. Don't get angry with cyclists even when they start acting like they own the road. Don't spit on cars. Don't drag race with strangers at night. Don't spin the back of your car out on deserted streets when there is a little moisture on the road surface. Don't drive cars with unneccesarily oversized engines when we are clearly running out of oil so fast. Don't drive too fast. Don't get involved in road-rage incidents if you are not a good fighter in real life. Don't get complacent. Don't imagine that a six lane highway is actually an arcade game. Don't judge people by the car that they drive. Don't drive an ugly car. Don't drive drunk. Don't make excuses. Don't watch too much TV. Don't berate the advert breaks if you are in anyway involved with them. Don't stop reading books. Don't forget that fiction is not real. Don't get obsessed with things for too long. Don't feel it is acceptable to be racist toward countries and their people just because they have the same skin color as you. Don't casually address your friends with terms that were once used as derogatory monikers for ethnic minorities even if the aforementioned friends are descendants of the relevant minority and use the term in a friendly way towards you. Don't become obsessed with the cleanliness of your living space to the point where you can no longer function easily within it. Don't go for more than seventy two hours without a shower where possible. Don't have showers or baths when showing the early symptoms of a cold or the flu. Don't think it is acceptable to cease communicating with your grandparents because they don't have e-mail. Don't think that older generations aren't extremely wise and knowledgeable just because they don't share the same vernacular. Don't get hung up about age. Don't judge achievements by the age at which they were achieved. Don't be scared of getting old. Don't be scared to die. Don't write songs about your mother. Don't let male singers sing backing lyrics on hip hop tracks. Don't be homophobic. Don't be offended if you are playing music at a wedding and an elderly guest asks you if you have any white music. Don't lie out in the sun until you get burnt. Don't use a suntan as an aesthetic ballast for a paunch. Don't stop swimming in the ocean through an irrational fear of sharks. Don't mistake dolphins as sharks. Don't tell your partner that dolphins are sharks. Don't be sarcastic. Don't try and avoid commitment without good reason. Don't fart in bed. Don't encourage others to fart in bed. Don't smoke cigarettes after you have brushed your teeth even though it tastes nice and helps you sleep. Don't be afraid to use existing work as inspiration as long as you are sure you are making a progression. Don't be mortified to see that someone else has already had that idea. Don't read the trade press. Don't idolise people. Don't underestimate the power of PR. Don't think that people do it on their own. Don't use jargon. Don't use analogies that position yourself alongside Mondrian. Don't think about obituaries. Don't judge progress using people you have never met as a barometer. Don't stop writing letters. Don't compose a letter in your head more than five times without actually writing it and sending it. Don't write letters that you have been procrastinating over for more than a year. Don't text drunk. Don't attempt to be humourous in professional e-mail correspondence. Don't let typographic sensibilities negate the potential to respond to a mundane e-mail in under five minutes. Don't pinch girls. Don't swear as much. Don't get into fights. Don't go out with wet hair. Don't sneeze in public in Japan. Don't break any bones showing off. Don't ignore important global issues. Don't be rude about people you know unless they are with you at the time. Don't over think things. Don't sweat profusely in important meetings. Don't shout at trees and plants. Don't think about money a lot. Don't stop allocating at least a few minutes a week to planning what you would spend the lottery jackpot on should the ticket you never buy win. Don't think so much about which type of food you would eat if someone said you could now only eat one type of food for the rest of your life. Don't just take digital photos. Don't forget to do what you told everyone you were going to. Don't make too many lists. Don't believe the hype.

Design   Angus Hyland / Pentagram
Project   I Am Type
Category   Poster
Date   2003

For an exhibition called 'Public Address System' 40 designers were asked to create a poster that interpreted a public speech of their choice, ranging from great political addresses to lyrics from a song. The exhibition was organized by the Henry Peacock Gallery and *Grafik* magazine. This poster includes 27 quotes from an array of graphic-design luminaries, with one from Frederic Goudy from 1927 pulled out in red. Set all in caps, it translucently overprints the other smaller quotations, and breaks out of the white rectangle that confines the rest of the text.

Design   Struktur Design
Project   K Not C, No E
Category   Poster
Date   2001

To promote a talk by Roger Fawcett-Tang at the London College of Printing, this poster plays with a phonetic version of 'radio speak' (a = alpha, z = zulu). The title 'K Not C, No E' refers to the spelling of 'Struktur' which uses the Danish as opposed to the English spelling – so a 'k' replaces the 'c' and there is no 'e' on the end. The clean simple typography helps to focus attention on the unfamiliar words and letters.

Design	Struktur Design with Sean Lewis
Project	In Alphabetical Order
Category	Poster
Date	2003

Twenty-six ISTD members were paired with members of the writers' professional body 26 and given a brief to produce a poster taking as its starting point a letter of the alphabet. Given the letter 'a', writer Sean Lewis suggested the idea of alphabetical listings and the potential advantages of being first in a list. The designer's solution was to generate a clean, simple poster that highlights the alphabetical sequence in the title, in which the letters 'a', 'b', 'c', 'd' and 'e' are picked out in alphabetical order.

Design	Stapelberg & Fritz
Project	AM7
Category	Journal promotional poster
Date	2001

To promote their design for a German journal, Stapelberg & Fritz used a running sheet of the publication's cover section and overprinted a contents list and information about the journal on it in black. The bold all-caps Akzidenz Grotesk type is reversed out of a black rectangle, allowing fragments of the cover section to be revealed.

Design   Experimental Jetset
Project   De Theater Compagnie
Category   Visual identity / posters
Date   2005

A very simple typographic solution was adopted for the
visual identity and printed matter for this Dutch theatre
company. Each play is advertised using the same sans-serif
font and a simple colour palette (black, white and one other
colour). However, the typography is treated in a playful
manner, at times similar to the concrete poetry of the 1960s.

Design	Stapelberg & Fritz
Project	12inch Club
Category	Club flyers
Date	2005

A series of monthly flyers were produced for this German nightclub. Square to reflect the format of a record sleeve, they use bold Neue Helvetica throughout, with the month printed large across each one – the word is broken up to reveal other words such as 'ok', 'ember' and 'ja!'. Although the club's name remains in the same position on each flyer, the other information playfully moves around from month to month.

Design	Wim Crouwel
Project	Dutch Pavilion
Category	Poster
Date	2005

To promote a film installation by the artist duo Jeroen de Rijke and Willem de Rooij for the Dutch Pavilion at the 51st Venice Biennale, the designer produced a poster based on a simple typographic play on the artists' names, with the two 'de R's mirroring each other. A strong dynamic is created by the off-centre placement.

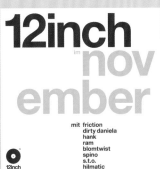

Design	Experimental Jetset
Project	SMCS
Category	Visual identity / printed matter
Date	2004

The designers created a complete graphic identity system
for Stedelijk Museum CS, the temporary exhibition space of
the Amsterdam museum of modern art. This included
logotype, signage system, bimonthly magazine and
exhibition posters. The identity renders the letters (set in
a bold sans-serif font) in a series of diagonal lines in cyan
and red. This diagonal line is used throughout the other
applications together with the clean sans font printed in
cyan and red.

Stedelijk Museum CS

Stedelijk Museum CS

16.05 31.12
Tussenstand:
een keuze uit de
collectie
Intermission:
a choice from the
collection

16.05 03.10
20/20 Vision
Yesim Akdeniz Graf,
Francis Alÿs, Marc
Bijl, Germaine Kruip,
De Rijke / De Rooij,
Mathias Poledna,
Steve McQueen,
Torbjørn Rødland

16.05 29.08
Kramer vs. Rietveld
/Contrasten in
de meubelcollectie
Kramer vs. Rietveld
/Contrasts in the
furniture collection

www.stedelijk.nl

Stedelijk Museum CS
Oosterdokskade 5
1011 AD Amsterdam

Dagelijks open: 10-18 uur
Donderdag: 10-21 uur
Open daily: 10 am-6 pm
Thursday: 10 am-9 pm

Verwacht: Best Verzorgde
Boeken, Prix de Rome,
Sandberg, Gemeente Kunst
Aankopen, Who If Not We,
Robert Smit & Gold, IDFA

Expected: Best Book Design,
Prix de Rome, Sandberg,
Municipal Art Acquisitions,
Who If Not We, Robert Smit
& Gold, IDFA

Meubelindustrie
Gelderland BV
Mondriaan Stichting

Gemeente
Amsterdam
Economische Zaken

20 20 √vision

Yesim Akdeniz Graf
Francis Alÿs
Marc Bijl
Germaine Kruip

Steve McQueen
Mathias Poledna
De Rijke/De Rooij
Torbjørn Rødland

16.05 - 03.10.2004
Stedelijk Museum CS
Oosterdokskade 5
1011 AD Amsterdam

20 20 √vision

Design	Studio von Birken
Project	Janou Pakter
Category	Brochure
Date	2005

A playful use of Bodoni is featured in this project for an international executive recruitment agency. The oversized thick card cover contains a delicate brochure printed in just black and white. The text pages use a very light weight of paper which allows a high level of translucency. This helps to build interesting typographic constructions from the different headlines throughout the brochure. The body text is printed in a light weight of Futura; indeed, it is so light it almost disappears.

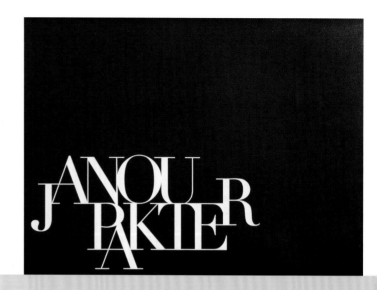

Design — Cartlidge Levene
Project — Bruce Nauman: Raw Materials
Category — Book
Date — 2004

Produced to accompany a large-scale sound installation by Bruce Nauman in the Turbine Hall at Tate Modern, London, this book is broken into three clear sections. The first contains a series of essays, the second prints the transcripts of all the words and phrases used in the sound installation – these transcripts range from short stories to single words which are repeated over and over on the page. The final section is printed in full colour and shows a selection of Nauman's other works and images, plus preparatory sketches for the Turbine Hall installation. The same serif font is used throughout.

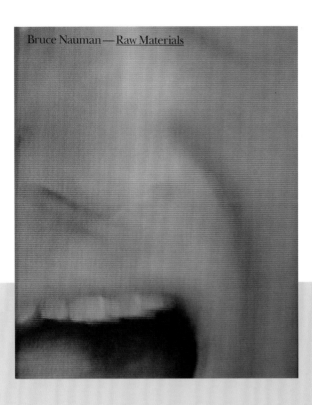

Bruce Nauman — Raw Materials

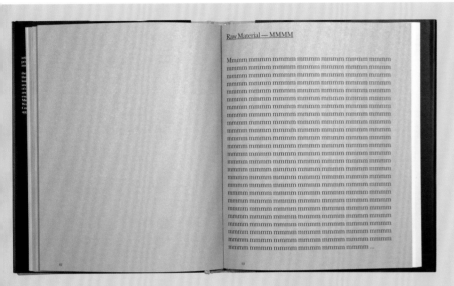

Raw Material — MMMM

Mmmm mmmm mmmm mmmm mmmm mmmm mmmm
mmmm mmmm mmmm mmmm mmmm mmmm mmmm
mmmm mmmm mmmm mmmm mmmm mmmm mmmm
mmmm mmmm mmmm mmmm mmmm mmmm mmmm
mmmm mmmm mmmm mmmm mmmm mmmm mmmm
mmmm mmmm mmmm mmmm mmmm mmmm mmmm
mmmm mmmm mmmm mmmm mmmm mmmm mmmm
mmmm mmmm mmmm mmmm mmmm mmmm mmmm
mmmm mmmm mmmm mmmm mmmm mmmm mmmm
mmmm mmmm mmmm mmmm mmmm mmmm mmmm
mmmm mmmm mmmm mmmm mmmm mmmm mmmm
mmmm mmmm mmmm mmmm mmmm mmmm mmmm
mmmm mmmm mmmm mmmm mmmm mmmm mmmm
mmmm mmmm mmmm mmmm mmmm mmmm mmmm
mmmm mmmm mmmm mmmm mmmm mmmm mmmm
mmmm mmmm mmmm mmmm mmmm mmmm mmmm
mmmm mmmm mmmm mmmm mmmm mmmm mmmm
mmmm mmmm mmmm mmmm mmmm mmmm mmmm
mmmm mmmm mmmm mmmm mmmm mmmm mmmm
mmmm mmmm mmmm mmmm mmmm mmmm mmmm
mmmm mmmm mmmm mmmm mmmm mmmm mmmm
mmmm mmmm mmmm mmmm mmmm mmmm mmmm
mmmm mmmm mmmm mmmm mmmm mmmm mmmm
mmmm mmmm mmmm mmmm mmmm mmmm mmmm
mmmm mmmm mmmm mmmm mmmm mmmm mmmm ...

OK OK OK

OK OK OK OK OK OK OK OK OK OK OK OK OK OK OK OK OK
OK OK OK OK OK OK OK OK OK OK OK OK OK OK OK OK OK
OK OK OK OK OK OK OK OK OK OK OK OK OK OK OK OK OK ...

Think Think Think

Think think think think think think think think think think
think think think think think think think think think think think ...

Catalogue Entries
Ben Borthwick

Design	A2/SW/HK
Project	Dan Fern: Walks with Colour
Category	Book
Date	2006

This elegant book showcases recent paintings by the artist Dan Fern. The designers created a lovely serif font specifically for the publication. Used large on the introductory essay pages, the font readily reveals its quirky nature. The italic font includes some unusual ligatures, such as 'gi', 'si', 'st', 'ff', 'ct' and 'ch'. The essay section is followed by the plates, which are hand-tipped in. As an interlude, a series of the artist's poems are inserted halfway through on half-width pages of a different stock.

2.35 pm. The tide is far enough out and it seems we can continue to Birling Gap after all. It means another two miles of arduous, unsteady hiking. We are alone on the beach.

3.25 pm. At last we are back on the cliffs. We have walked about 11 miles and my legs know it. The light is already fading and we will have to abandon the plan to complete the walk with a detour through Friston Forest, since we don't have a torch. We walk back over the Sisters and then strike out across the fields to find the road that leads back to Fern's car.

In our conversations, Fern has been modest in the claims he makes for his recent pieces. I am curious to know whether he sees them as works of art.

"They are quiet thoughts rather than a grand statement," he says. "I guess it's more natural to talk of them in terms of meditations or stillnesses than anything too exalted. Mind that -" He points out a cowpat. "I really feel that I'm starting to arrive at something that pulls together all the things I'm interested in - intellectually, physically and emotionally - into something which, for me anyway, works."

"A lot of these new images were inspired by the French landscape. Do you want viewers to read and understand them in this way? Should they be thinking of landscape?"

"Yes, I think they should, actually. I didn't think that to begin with. I thought I'd like them to be completely abstract. I don't want them to be seen as pictorial representations of landscape, but they were definitely inspired by landscape and by being in the landscape and I have no problem with people reading them in that way."

The field we are crossing in the grey light is full of cows. Some are mooing.

"It's like saying, 'I've been walking all day and I saw these colours together.' It's as simple as that. I thought they were beautiful. I've tried to record them. Not exactly, of course, but something of the sense of enjoyment that one gets from seeing certain colour combinations. You try to duplicate that or relive it. They are, for me, very much evocations of a certain place and inspired directly by specific locations. I title sets of pictures by the places that inspired them and that is as far as I need to go."

12   13

Dan Fern

WALKS WITH COLOUR

Recent Works
on Paper

Edited by Rick Poynor

List of works

Diois Series

Vercheny Series

Haiku Series

183

Design	Ph.D
Project	Terms and Conditions
Category	Book
Date	2004

Produced to celebrate the company's 16th anniversary, this small pocketbook contains 39 dictionary-style entries. Each definition is treated in a different typographic manner, all printed in orange and black and set in a variety of different typefaces including Franklin Gothic, Clarendon, Gill Sans, Meta and Din.

Design	Design Project
Project	Situation Leeds: Contemporary Artists and the Public Realm 05 05
Category	Catalogue
Date	2005

The title effectively starts on the back of this pre-folded festival guide and runs round onto the front of the booklet. Printed on an uncoated pink stock in fluorescent pink and silver, the strong bold Futura typography is accompanied by a simplified graphic map of the city centre in fluorescent orange on the cover. At the centre of the booklet a more detailed map is bound in, with all the locations for the various events highlighted.

Form
36

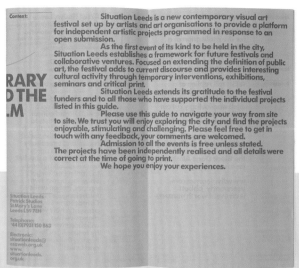

Free · Festival guide May 16 to 29 2005

SITUATION LEEDS: CONTEMPORARY ARTISTS AND THE PUBLIC REALM 05 05

01 41:
Festival projects

42 47:
Talks

48 50:
Future projects

51 60:
Related projects

Context:

Situation Leeds is a new contemporary visual art festival set up by artists and art organisations to provide a platform for independent artistic projects programmed in response to an open submission.

As the first event of its kind to be held in the city, Situation Leeds establishes a framework for future festivals and collaborative ventures. Focused on extending the definition of public cultural activity through temporary interventions, exhibitions, seminars and critical print.

Situation Leeds extends its gratitude to the festival funders and to all those who have supported the individual projects listed in this guide.

Please use this guide to navigate your way from site to site. We trust you will enjoy exploring the city and find the projects enjoyable, stimulating and challenging. Please feel free to get in touch with any feedback, your comments are welcomed.

Admission to all the events is free unless stated. The projects have been independently realised and all details were correct at the time of going to print.

We hope you enjoy your experiences.

Situation Leeds
Patrick Studios
St Mary's Lane
Leeds LS9 7EH

Telephone:
+44 (0)7931 150 863

Electronic:
situationleeds@
ncoweb.org.uk
www.
situationleeds.
org.uk

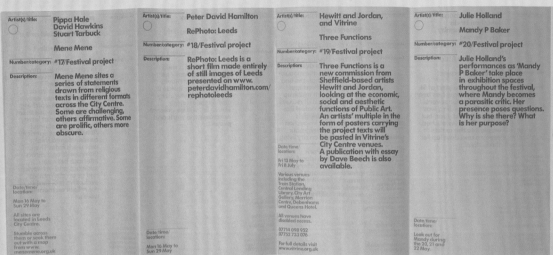

Artist(s)/title:	Pippa Hale, David Hawkins, Stuart Tarbuck
	Mene Mene
Number/category:	#17/Festival project
Description:	Mene Mene sites a series of statements drawn from religious texts in different formats across the City Centre. Some are challenging, others affirmative. Some are prolific, others more obscure.
Date/time/location:	Mon 16 May to Sun 29 May. All sites are located in Leeds City Centre. Shamble across them or seek them out with a map from www.menexene.org.uk

Artist(s)/title:	Peter David Hamilton
	RePhoto: Leeds
Number/category:	#18/Festival project
Description:	RePhoto: Leeds is a short film made entirely of still images of Leeds presented on www.peterdavidhamilton.com/rephotoleeds
Date/time/location:	Mon 16 May to Sun 29 May

Artist(s)/title:	Hewitt and Jordan, and Vitrine
	Three Functions
Number/category:	#19/Festival project
Description:	Three Functions is a new commission from Sheffield-based artists Hewitt and Jordan, looking at the economic, social and aesthetic functions of Public Art. An artists' multiple in the form of posters carrying the project texts will be pasted in Vitrine's City Centre venues. A publication with essay by Dave Beech is also available.
Date/time/location:	Fri 13 May to Fri 8 July. Various venues including the Train Station, Central Lending Library, City Art Gallery, Merrion Centre, Debenhams and Queens Hotel. All venues have disabled access. 07714 098 952 07752 733 076 for full details visit www.vitrine.org.uk

Artist(s)/title:	Julie Holland
	Mandy P Baker
Number/category:	#20/Festival project
Description:	Julie Holland's performances as 'Mandy P Baker' take place in exhibition spaces throughout the festival, where Mandy becomes a parasitic critic. Her presence poses questions. Why is she there? What is her purpose?
Date/time/location:	Look out for Mandy during the 20, 21 and 22 May.

Artist(s)/title:	Nichola Pemberton
	Over Hearing
Number/category:	#29/Festival project
Description:	Based on customer conversations this scripted performance piece is read by four actors. Not presented obviously, it mimics regular customers leaving the viewer to experience the café and wonder which overheard conversations are contrived.
Date/time/location:	Mon 23 May to Fri 27 May 2:30 – 3:30pm. Four Cousins Grille and Coffee Lounge 10 Market St Arcade Leeds LS1 6DH

Locator map:

Please use this map as a quick reference guide. Addresses for all projects are listed in this guide but if you require more detailed directions please refer to an A to Z of Leeds or visit streetmap.co.uk

For your reference, the festival projects listed below are situated outside the City Centre and do not appear on the locator map. For further info on these locations please see the address details listed in this guide.

05 Hyde Park
07 Brahm Gallery
21 LEDA
25 Lotherton Hall
35 Back Newton Grove
36 Cookridge Info Centre
40 Unit Café Bar
48 Pinderfields General Hospital
56 Leeds Industrial Museum

Please note that some projects do not have set venues or venue details and therefore are not listed here.

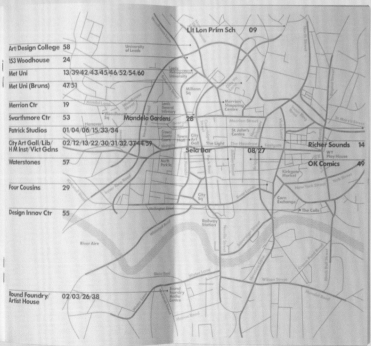

Art/Design College	58
153 Woodhouse	24
Met Uni	13/39 42 43 45 46 52 54 60
Met Uni (Bruns)	47 51
Merrion Ctr	19
Swarthmore Ctr	53
Patrick Studios	01/04 06 15 33/34
City Art Gall/Lib/ H M Inst/Vict Gdns	02/12 13 22 30/31 32 37/41 59
Waterstones	57
Four Cousins	29
Design Innov Ctr	55
Round Foundry/ Artist House	02/03 26/38

Lit Lon Prim Sch 09
Richer Sounds 14
OK Comics 49

Design	Cartlidge Levene
Project	The Business of Design: Design Industry Research 2005
Category	Brochure
Date	2005

This elegant research handbook converts what could be very dry information into a rich, colourful document. The cover features a string of statistics printed in a combination of magenta and white out of red bars which run vertically up the page. Inside, the clean sans-serif typography is combined with handwritten text on the divider pages.

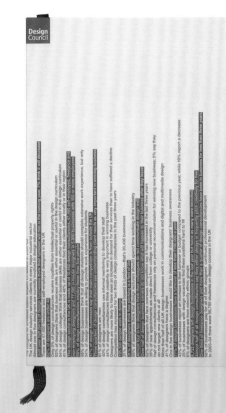

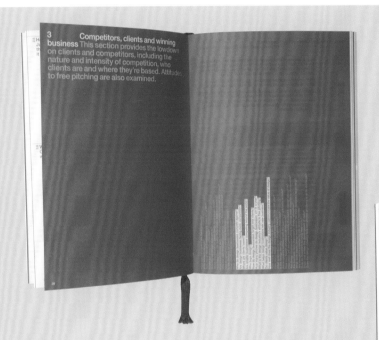

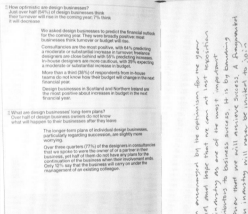

Design	David Jury
Project	Humphrey Spender: Morocco: A Desert Adventure
Category	Book
Date	2004

A lavish limited-edition letterpress volume which recalls the travels through Morocco in the 1930s by the English photojournalist Humphrey Spender. The book features transcripts of Spender's original diary entries made during the trip alongside the edited version he produced on his return to England. The text is set as a series of parallel columns, with the edited version printed on the left in Monotype Baskerville, and the original version printed on the right in Monotype Grotesque. A natural typographic rhythm is formed by these parallel columns which begin and end at arbitrary positions, creating unusual white spaces within the columns.

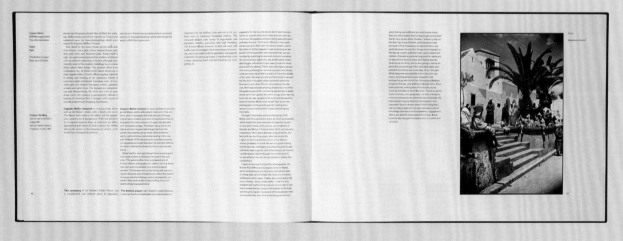

Design	Browns
Project	Northsoutheastwest: A 360° View of Climate Change
Category	Book
Date	2005

Produced for the British Council and the Climate Change Group, this beautiful, photography-heavy book captures the devastating effects of climate change on the natural environment. The minimal typographic cover plays with the orientation of the book. Inside, all text and images run at 90 degrees to the spine. The bold condensed sans serif used for all the titling, printed in red, black and grey, creates a strong presence on the page.

Design	Projekttriangle
Project	IAD Interaction Design
Category	Brochure
Date	2004

Playing with the visual language of screen-based graphics, this brochure builds on a basic CAD aesthetic. A series of axometric cubes are grouped together to form the title of the workshop, which creates a 3D axometric dot-matrix font. The same font is converted into 2D and used inside the brochure for page numbers. This is supplemented by a more conventional OCR-style font for all the main text setting.

PHYSICAL ENVIRONMENT
DEVELOPMENT
NATURAL ENVIRONMENT
HUMAN RIGHTS
TECHNOLOGY
FOOD
HEALTH
URBAN LIFE
ECONOMY
LEADERSHIP

GREENLAND
SOUTH AFRICA
KENYA
MARSHALL ISLANDS
JAPAN
CHINA
INDIA
MEXICO CITY
CALIFORNIA
UK/GERMANY/NYC

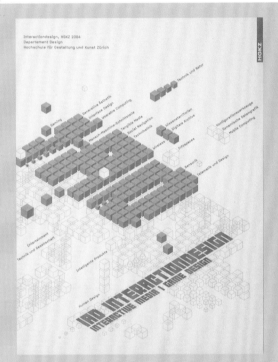

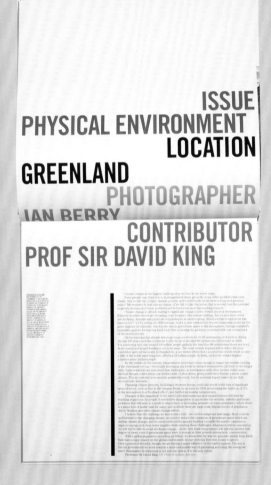

ISSUE
PHYSICAL ENVIRONMENT
LOCATION
GREENLAND
PHOTOGRAPHER
IAN BERRY
CONTRIBUTOR
PROF SIR DAVID KING

WEST
NORTH
SOUTH
EAST

Design	Browns
Project	Bruce Gilden: A Beautiful Catastrophe
Category	Book
Date	2005

The title of this book by Magnum photographer Bruce Gilden is illustrated by the designers' typographic approach, with the letters ranged hard right against the edge of the book, forcing the final characters of the words onto the next line. A series of quotes are printed in a bold condensed American football-style font throughout the book. All leading has been removed to the extent that each line of type touches the next, which creates jarring negative space around the words.

Design	Projekttriangle
Project	RAM
Category	Poster / mailer
Date	2006

Printed on a thin bible paper, this poster uses a light angular sans-serif font to promote an exhibition of the designer's work. One side features a full-bleed image of a girl wearing a headset. The reverse, text-based side is printed in red, green and blue in a reference to the primary screen-based colour palette. The use of a translucent stock means that the title of the exhibition is partially visible on the image side of the poster.

Form
40

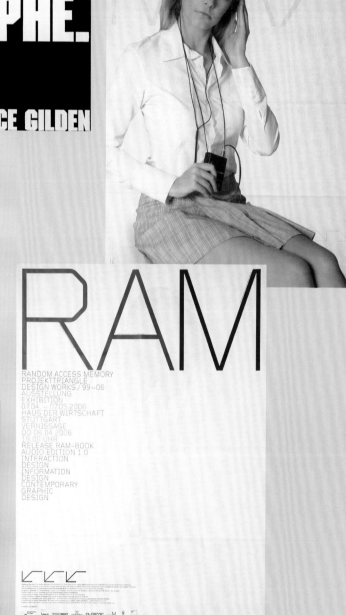

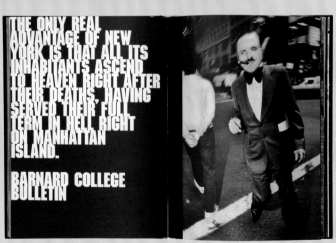

Design	RBG6
Project	UNG 06/07
Category	Poster / catalogue jacket
Date	2006

UNG 06/07 is a perennial juried travelling exhibition featuring young Swedish design talent. The designers have created a visual concept for all related items, from the call for entries poster to the website and exhibition catalogue as well as invitation cards and diplomas which are created from overprinted copies of the poster cut down to size. The poster is also used for the jacket of the catalogue, with an extra image printed on the reverse.

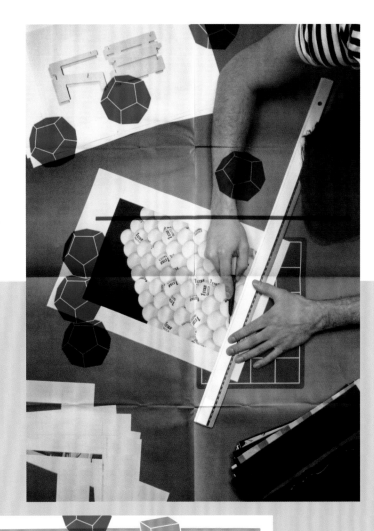

Design	Intégral Ruedi Baur et Associés
Project	Cinémathèque Française
Category	Visual identity
Date	2005

The identity for the French cinema museum is based on projected light, the very essence of cinema. A series of overlapping angled projections of light provide overall definition. The bold monospaced sans-serif font gives a strong, clearly legible focus to the subtle light projections.

AU 51 RUE DE BERCY
Ouverture le 28 septembre 2005

À LA CINÉMATHÈQUE FRANÇAISE

14000m²
Quatre salles de projection
Des expositions temporaires
Les expositions permanentes
Des ateliers pédagogiques
Une librairie
Un restaurant
La Bibliothèque du Film

La Cinémathèque française est une association
loi 1901 subventionnée par le Ministère de la culture
et de la communication via le CNC, Centre national
de la cinématographie

LA CINÉMATHÈQUE FRANÇAISE

LA CINÉMATHÈQUE FRANÇAISE

51 RUE DE BERCY
75012 PARIS

WWW.CINEMATHEQUE.FR

Design	Surface
Project	The Forsythe Company
Category	Posters
Date	2006

This series of posters for the Forsythe Company combines manipulated overlaid images of the dancers with typographic distortions of the company's name which echo the dynamics of the bodies. The campaign revolves around the idea of non-dimensional space, its abstraction emphasized by the collaging process. The logo appears as a spatial element in different situations as well as being a dynamic, integrated part of the collage itself.

Design	RBG6
Project	Everything Useful Is Ugly
Category	Poster
Date	2002

Part of the graphic identity for the Konstfack BA graduate exhibition at the Kulturhuset, Stockholm in 2002, this simple typographic poster uses a bold cut of Futura, simply printed black on white. Incorporating virtually no other visual material, the poster is the essence of nothing. But the sheer scale of the typography combined with careful positioning and the introduction of a couple of triangular arrow cursors turns what could be a piece of 'non-design' into a considered statement.

Design	RBG6
Project	Edsvik Konsthall – Arghh
Category	Poster
Date	2003

This poster for an exhibition entitled 'Arghh' at the Edsvik Konsthall in Sweden again keeps to a very simple black-and-white dynamic using strong, bold typography. The unusual font combined with the triangular speech marks make for a striking poster.

Design	Research Studios
Project	Who's Next
Category	Visual identity / printed matter
Date	2003

Visual identity and art direction for 'Who's Next', a French
fashion show that has become one of the top international
events. Fragments of headline text set in Neue Helvetica
have been cut up and pasted onto the spreads. These cut-
ups give the pages a contemporary punk-aesthetic twist.

Design	Stiletto
Project	As Four Denim
Category	Visual identity / printed matter
Date	2005

Part of a visual identity for the New York-based fashion label As Four, this catalogue for the spring/summer denim collection sets the page numbers at a large scale compared with the rest of the information. The bold use of Akzidenz Grotesk endows the catalogue with a very modern feel.

Design	Studio Thomson
Project	Aquascutum Spring/Summer 2006
Category	Poster / invite
Date	2006

This small poster (A3 folded to A5) feels much larger than it actually is as a result of the designers scaling the type in such a way that it bleeds off all sides. The company's name is printed on one side of a thin translucent bible paper, while 'SS06' appears in a mirror image on the reverse – the designers make full use of the show-through effect. The typeface is a bold sans serif, infilled with what look like black-and-white photographs of the sea. The ripples of the water are echoed in the irregular edges of the font.

Design	Stiletto
Project	Ultrabland
Category	Visual identity / printed matter
Date	2004

The visual identity for this New York-based post-production video facility is set in a bold weight of Univers. In a play on the company's name, the logo deliberately teeters on the edge of blandness, an effect that is countered by the purity of the typography. A bright orange band is used to bind the folder and slices through the large-format logo. The band is also a visual reference to the tape used in editing suites.

Design	Substance®
Project	Dialogue: Ashbury / DJ Shang Hai
Category	Leaflet
Date	2005

Printed in one colour on dark Manilla card, this leaflet reproduces a transcription of an interview between two musicians using a clean grid system and pure modernist typography. The dialogue is printed on both sides of the leaflet, in a large point size on the right side of the page, with background information appearing on the left in a smaller size.

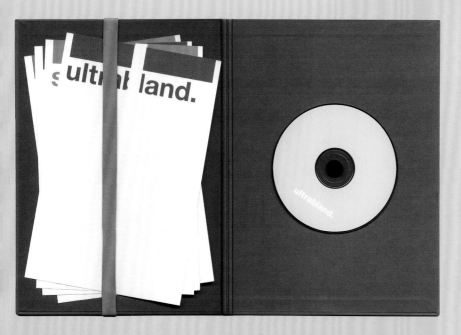

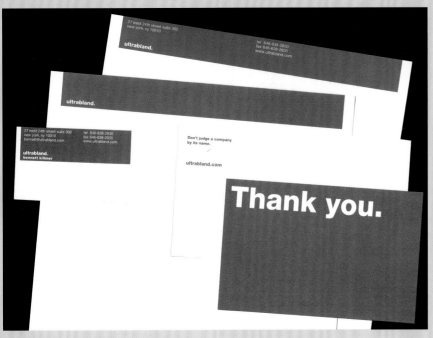

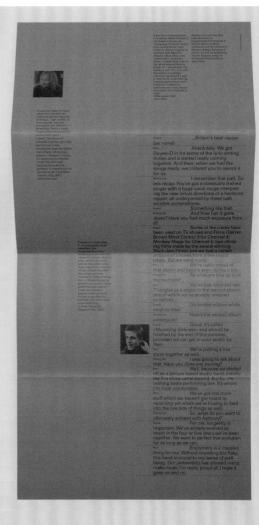

Design	CHK Design
Project	Miser & Now
Category	Magazine
Date	2005

The masthead of this contemporary art magazine is set in
a pastiche of traditional German blackletter Gothic
complete with swirly calligraphic marks. The logo is very
much at odds with the cover image and contents. More
contemporary fonts are used inside but still in a loose
and playful manner – which gives the magazine a slightly
anarchic feel.

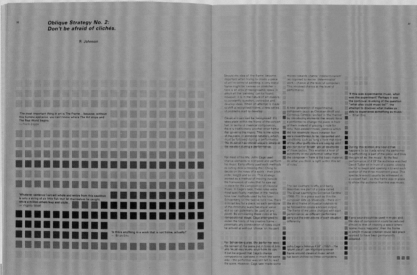

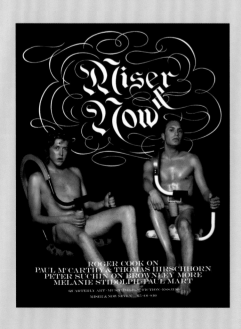

Design	George&Vera
Project	Fred
Category	Posters
Date	2005

The designers created a series of typographic posters for Fred, a London-based art gallery. Each plays with a different typographic theme, such as cropping (below) and repetition (bottom). The cropped poster has a list of performers printed in Neue Helvetica bold: the text is ranged left and starts from the centre of the poster. The words 'Playcolt' and 'MainOnes' bleed off the right edge and reappear bleeding in from the left edge. If several of these posters are hung side by side, the headline creates a bigger impact, since it can be read in a straightforward linear manner across the display.

Design	Exposure
Project	UK Film Council: Break-Through Brits
Category	Poster
Date	2005

This simple poster, produced to celebrate new British filmmaking talent in the USA, plays with a graphic interpretation of celluloid passing through the spools of a projector – note the use of the circular counters of the 'a', 'o' and 'g' in the bold Futura headline. The journey of the thin black line of film across the poster surface is extended through a series of white circles, which are the same size as the full stop on the headline font.

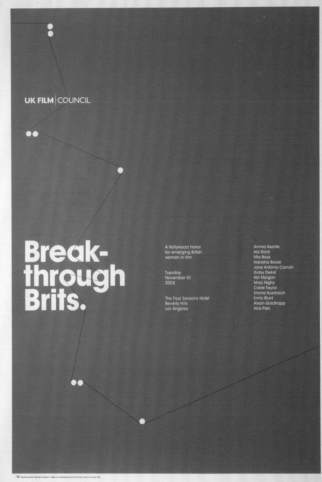

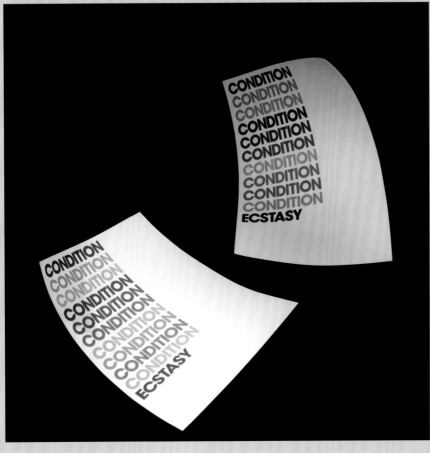

Design	A2/SW/HK
Project	Aveny-T
Category	Visual identity / posters
Date	2005

The custom-designed bold sans font gives the promotional posters for this Danish contemporary theatre a very distinctive look, even when they individually use such widely different imagery. The font – especially the letter 'J' – has the feel of a hand-drawn Bauhaus face. The edges of the letterforms have a natural look, as if they had been printed using woodblock type. It's not an easy feel to achieve with the crisp computer-controlled output of today.

Form
50

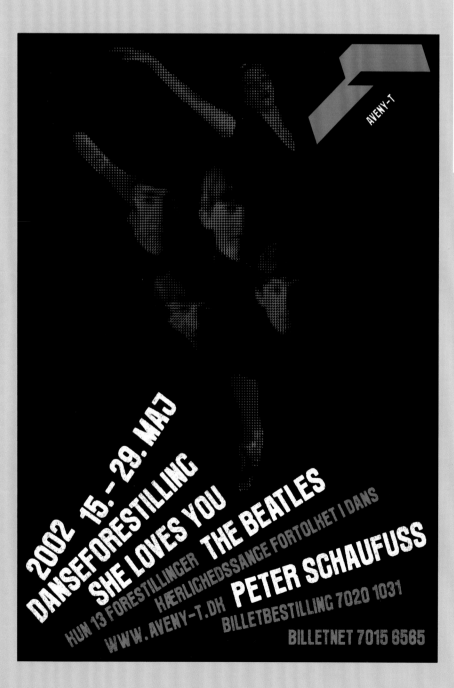

Design	Aufuldish & Warinner
Project	California College of the Arts
Category	Posters
Date	2005

These two posters for the California College of the Arts offer a total contrast. The typography on the bright and cheerful 'National Portfolio Day' poster is ranged left and printed very close to the trimmed edge. The blocks of colour behind each line of type are at odds with the slightly childlike quality of the illustrations. The stark black-and-white severity of the 'Architecture Lecture Series' poster, meanwhile, displays a recognizably American typographic aesthetic, combining a variety of different faces and heavy rules to give the overall design a very claustrophobic feel.

California College of the Arts hosts
National Portfolio Day NPDA
Saturday, January 15, 2005
At the CCA
San Francisco campus
1111 Eighth Street

Tours and financial aid workshops, 10 AM–noon
Portfolio reviews, noon–4 PM

CALIFORNIA COLLEGE OF THE ARTS
ARCHITECTURE PROGRAM
1111 EIGHTH STREET
SAN FRANCISCO, CA 94107-2247   CCA

CCA ARCHITECTURE LECTURE SERIES SPRING 2005

/01/31/ STEPHANE PRATTE / ATELIER IN SITU

/02/07/ DETLEF MERTINS / UNIVERSITY OF PENNSYLVANIA

/02/14/ JOHANNA GRAWUNDER / MILAN, SAN FRANCISCO

/02/21/ MICHAEL SPEAKS / SOUTHERN CALIFORNIA INSTITUTE OF ARCHITECTURE

/02/28/ MARCELO SPINA / PATTERNS

/03/07/ SULAN KOLATAN / KOL/MAC STUDIO

/03/28/ CHRISTOS MARCOPOULOS & CAROL MOUKHEIBER / STUDIO (N-1)

/04/04/ LISA FINDLEY / CALIFORNIA COLLEGE OF THE ARTS

/04/11/ AN TE LIU / UNIVERSITY OF TORONTO

/04/18/ ANTHONY BURKE / UC BERKELEY

WE WOULD LIKE TO ACKNOWLEDGE THE GENEROUS SUPPORT OF DONORS TO THE ARCHITECTURE LECTURE SERIES IN THE LAST TWELVE MONTHS. TITANIUM LEVEL: GRANTS FOR THE ARTS/SAN FRANCISCO HOTEL TAX FUND; LEF FOUNDATION. GRANITE LEVEL: GORDON H. CHONG & PARTNERS; JENSEN & MACY ARCHITECTS; MCCALL DESIGN GROUP. CONCRETE LEVEL: BARBARA SCAVULLO DESIGN; BEVERLY PRIOR ARCHITECTS; CCS ARCHITECTURE, INC.; DAVID BAKER + PARTNERS, ARCHITECTS; DONALD A. CROSBY, AIA; LEVY DESIGN PARTNERS; MBT ARCHITECTURE. TIMBER LEVEL: ELS ARCHITECTURE AND URBAN DESIGN; KAVA MASSIH ARCHITECTS. CCA WOULD ALSO LIKE TO THANK THE FOLLOWING FIRMS AND FOUNDATIONS FOR THEIR GENEROUS SUPPORT OF THE ARCHITECTURE PROGRAM: FONG & CHAN ARCHITECTS, GENSLER FAMILY FOUNDATION, LEF FOUNDATION, ANSHEN+ALLEN, GENSLER, IDEO, AND OVE ARUP AND PARTNERS CALIFORNIA LIMITED

All lectures Monday evenings at 7 PM in Timken Lecture Hall. Free and open to the public. Speakers are subject to change. For more information call 415.703.9562. CCA MONTGOMERY CAMPUS, 0000 EIGHTH STREET, SAN FRANCISCO.

Design	Eggers + Diaper
Project	Küba: Kutlug Ataman
Category	Book
Date	2005

Produced to accompany an installation by filmmaker Kutlug Ataman, featuring 40 old television sets, each showing a different filmed interview with inhabitants of Küba in Istanbul, the catalogue was designed as a kind of kitsch photo album to reflect something of the nature of the shanty town. The catalogue consists of a loose-leaf binder, finished in purple and deep red flocking, with the title foil-blocked in silver. Each of the 40 interviews is illustrated with photographs. The text is set in an old typewriter font, with corrections crossed out and overtyped. This gives the book a low-tech feel appropriate to the work.

Form

52

Design	MadeThought
Project	Established & Sons: 2005 Collection and 100% Design Tokyo
Category	Brochure
Date	2005

Two brochures produced for a contemporary British furniture manufacturer. The company's identity is formed by an odd typographic combination of a bold sans, an elaborate script and a bold 'poster' serif. This unusual mixture works to good effect in the brochures, where the bold serif bleeds off the page, giving the typographic treatment an illustrative quality.

'Osgerby/ ZERO-IN
Systems/ CHESTER
Hadid/AQUA TABLE
Holmes/ PINCH
el Marriott/ COURIER
der Taylor/ FOLD
ian Wrong/ CONVEX MIRROR
el Young/ WRITING DESK

Welcome to ESTABLISHED & SONS premier collection of furniture. The products shown here have been designed by a collective of Britain's most accomplished and inspiring designers.
They range from a remarkable table by illustrious architect Zaha Hadid to a handsome writing desk by Michael Young. There is an elegant, low table from BarberOsgerby and a covetable family of lamps from Alexander Taylor. Amanda Levete of Future Systems has created a contemporary take on the Chesterfield sofa and Mark Holmes a refined stackable chair. Sebastian Wrong has designed an extraordinary mirror and Michael Marriott a functional shelving system.
The sum of this first collection illustrates the breadth and quality of British design talent and offers a furniture solution for everybody.

Established & SONS
British Made

Michael Young / WRITING DESK

DESCRIPTION/
DESK WITH DRAWER
AND CONCEALED LIGHT
DIMENSIONS/
L1600MM x D680MM x H1150MM
MATERIALS/
FELT, ALUMINIUM,
WOOD CONGLOMERATE
COLOURS/
PALE GREEN AND CARDINAL RED,
BRAZIL BROWN AND CANTON BLUE

ED & SONS
INVITE
JAPANESE
THEIR
RNITURE
N IN TOKYO,
ER 2005

The comprehensive collection of ESTABLISHED & SONS production furniture will be exhibited to an Asian market at the first 100% Design show in Tokyo. A launch party will be held on the evening of Friday 4 November 2005 with DJ, bar and original installations. Established & Sons will launch their new, extensive website during the show.

Exhibition Dates
2 November – 6 November 2005

Established & SONS

D A PASSION
SIGN TALENT.
TELY
K, APPROACH
KEEPS THE

Design	A2/SW/HK
Project	Bongorama Productions
Category	Visual identity
Date	2005

Inspired by a beautiful old enamelled street sign in Denmark, the font makes the most of its quirky lowercase 'g' and even develops an interesting ligature for it. This identity for Bongorama Productions focuses on the company's initials, combining the 'B' and 'P' into a single letterform.

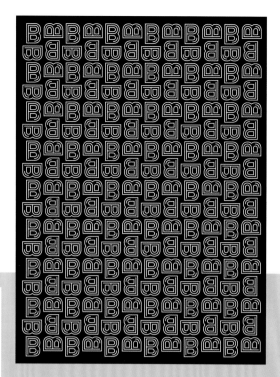

Form
54

ABC&DEFGHI|KLM
NOPQRSTUVWXYZÆØÅ
(1234£€567890)
abcdeffifflʆʓihijklmnop
qrsßtuvwxyzæøå
[{!+*@-/←♥→™✢¶®©]

Det er selskabets formål at udvikle og afvikle kulturbegivenheder med udgangspunkt i metropolen København. Kulturbegivenhederne skal drives af kunstnerisk kraft, æstetisk fornemmelse og teknisk kvalitet.

Det er selskabets formål at udvikle og afvikle kulturbegivenheder med udgangspunkt i metropolen København. Kulturbegivenhederne skal drives af kunstnerisk kraft, æstetisk fornemmelse og teknisk kvalitet.

Det er selskabets formål at udvikle og afvikle kulturbegivenheder med udgangspunkt i metropolen København. Kulturbegivenhederne skal drives af kunstnerisk kraft, æstetisk fornemmelse og teknisk kvalitet.

Det er selskabets formål at udvikle og afvikle kulturbegivenheder med udgangspunkt i metropolen København. Kulturbegivenhederne skal drives af kunstnerisk kraft, æstetisk fornemmelse og teknisk kvalitet.

Design	Laurenz Brunner
Project	Akkurat Specimen 1-7
Category	Font design / specimen book
Date	2005

This clean modern sans serif is firmly rooted in the tradition of Neue Helvetica, Akzidenz Grotesk and Univers. It comes in light, regular, bold and italic versions, with an added monospaced version of the regular weight. To promote the new family, the designer produced an elegant specimen book which comprises four folded posters, one for each weight. These sheets have been folded and cut along the central crease, allowing them to be read as conventional eight-page folded booklets as well as posters.

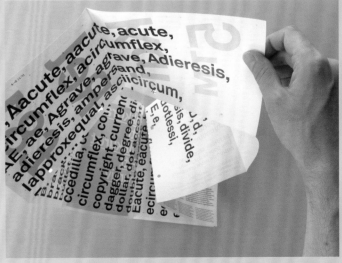

Design	Laurenz Brunner
Project	Gerrit Rietveld Academie
Category	Poster series
Date	2005

This series of posters for the graduation class from the Gerrit Rietveld Academie in Holland illustrates the extraordinary international mix of students at the college – 32 countries, 21 different languages. Each poster features text in Dutch plus at least one other language spoken at the college, with each language screenprinted in a different colour. Some of the posters were overprinted with several different languages, creating a very dense 'noise' of language, colour and type. The names of all the students are listed at the foot of the poster, with each one highlighted in the colour corresponding to his or her country of origin: Dutch in orange, Arabic in pink etc.

Design	Struktur Design
Project	Units
Category	Calendar
Date	2006

This project comprises two almost identical calendars, each showing the numerical sequence from 0 to 9, the only difference between the two parts being the colour sequence. The calendar strips back the information to an absolute minimum, allowing the user to experiment with the look of the calendar and its usage. A backing sheet contains all the dates for the year, including days, weeks and months, which means that the calendar can show the days (1–31), weeks (1–52) and months (1–12). Each number is die-cut from a different coloured sheet of card, which permits fragments of the next page in the numerical sequence to be visible.

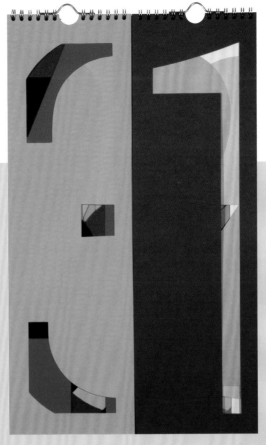

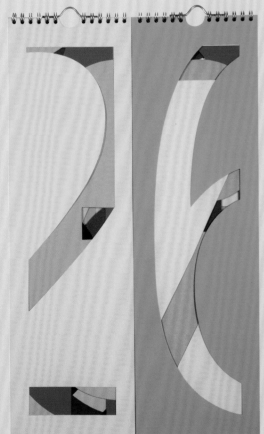

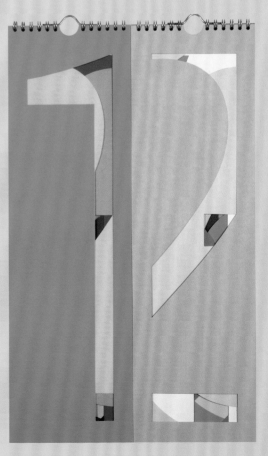

Design	Nokia Design Brand Team
Project	About Nokia
Category	Annual report
Date	2005

This annual report for the mobile phone company Nokia combines two different formats that carry different levels of information. The large French-folded pages feature a series of informal photographs of people printed onto a thin stock; a series of large typographic statements, some of which are printed in mirror image on the inside of the French-folded pages, are just legible through the light paper. A sequence of smaller pages are bound into the bottom of the brochure, printed on an uncoated stock, and feature the more conventional annual report information.

Design	Nokia Design Brand Team
Project	Nokia retail bags
Category	Carrier bags
Date	2005

As part of the extensive global branding exercise undertaken by Nokia, this range of carrier bags was developed using a purely typographic solution. A different bag has been created for every country in which the company operates. The country name and international dialling code are printed in the palette of Nokia brand colours around the bag, allowing only fragments of the type to be read on any one individual bag face.

Design	Nokia Design Brand Team
Project	Pure Ideas
Category	Brochures and posters
Date	2005

Produced as an internal document for the company, this brochure charts the work of the newly formed Nokia Design Brand Team. The brochure shows the corporate colours, typography, photographic treatments and graphic elements developed for the new branding system. Abstract typographic fragments are used to illustrate the new approach. A series of large folded posters was also produced, again using typographic fragments to show off the palette of colours developed for the company.

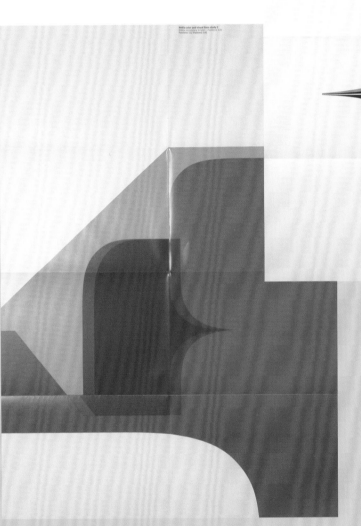

Design	Non–Format
Project	Back to Black
Category	Record packaging
Date	2005

Using a custom-drawn font, the designers let the super-bold filled-in font speak for itself on the two silkscreen-printed posters included in the gatefold sleeve. Having the title embossed into the plain gold-foiled cover adds a touch of bling to this limited-edition project.

Design	Saturday
Project	GQ Style
Category	Font / editorial design
Date	2005

A new headline font, Mattias, was created for the launch
of this magazine. The all-caps font is very heavy and totally
filled in, creating an impression of extreme solidity
on the printed page. Using the solid nature of the font, the
designers have playfully infilled the letterforms with images
to build up a picture (bottom).

Design	A2/SW/HK
Project	VogueOne
Category	Typeface
Date	2006

Based loosely on a modern serif font a bit like Bodoni, this typeface, created for British *Vogue*, features an array of flourishes and swirls. Variants are available for numerous characters, allowing headline setting to become far more playful and quirky. The addition of various ligatures makes for an excellent headline font, which can work at a clean formal level. Alternatively, by utilizing the alternative characters, it can become far more illustrative.

Design	A2/SW/HK
Project	VogueTwo
Category	Typeface
Date	2006

Based loosely on a modern serif font a bit like Bodoni Poster, this face, created for British *Vogue*, was designed as a purely uppercase font to accompany VogueOne. It has a heavier stroke, creating an extreme contrast between the thins and thicks.

VogueOne

COPYRIGHT A2/SW/HK LIMITED

BOLD

a
nautical
fantastic figure
amazing butterflies
style check
slight

❋

VogueTwo

COPYRIGHT A2/SW/HK LIMITED

BOLD

DR
EAM
S

VogueOne

COPYRIGHT A2/SW/HK LIMITED

BOLD

style
check
fantastic
figure

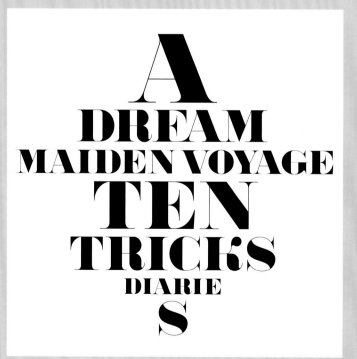

A
DREAM
MAIDEN VOYAGE
TEN
TRICKS
DIARIE
S

Design	Saturday
Project	Chenpascual
Category	Visual identity / printed matter
Date	2004

The designers extended the design of the logotype for this fashion label into a full typeface, with the typographic styling influencing all applications such as advertising and brochure design. The thin strokes of the serif font have been bleached out, resulting in a delicate face which seems to be fading from the surface. The graphic styling uses a lot of black, with the logo printed white out, which gives the effect of the black printing bleeding into the fine hairlines of the font.

Design	Studio von Birken
Project	Katja & Katia
Category	Magazine
Date	2005

Coarsely printed in black and white on low-grade newsprint, this biannual fashion magazine contrasts the high gloss of fashion with the disposability of a daily newspaper. The magazine is image-driven, except on the imprint page, which doubles as a preview for the next issue. Here a large bold Bodoni script is printed over the sans serif in a seemingly random fashion.

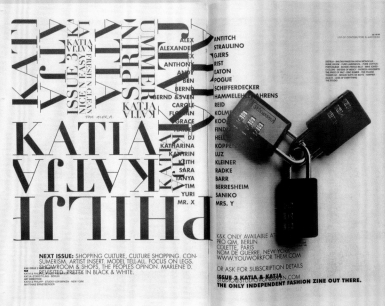

Design	Studio 3005
Project	OCW Talent
Category	Font design / book
Date	2005

OCW Talent was developed for the Dutch Ministry of Education, Culture and Science. The family consists of 18 different versions, including regular, bold and black, plus italics, old style figures (OSF) and small caps. Use of the typeface is restricted to the ministry. The small book *Museum als pretpark!* (The Museum as an Amusement Park!) demonstrates how well it works as a text face.

abcdefghijklmnopqrstuvwxyz
ABCDEFGHIJKLMNOPQRSTUVWXYZ
ABCDEFGHIJKLMNOPQRSTUVWXYZ
0123456789 0123456789

abcdefghijklmnopqrstuvwxyz
ABCDEFGHIJKLMNOPQRSTUVWXYZ
ABCDEFGHIJKLMNOPQRSTUVWXYZ
0123456789 0123456789

abcdefghijklmnopqrstuvwxyz
ABCDEFGHIJKLMNOPQRSTUVWXYZ
ABCDEFGHIJKLMNOPQRSTUVWXYZ
0123456789 0123456789

abcdefghijklmnopqrstuvwxyz
ABCDEFGHIJKLMNOPQRSTUVWXYZ
ABCDEFGHIJKLMNOPQRSTUVWXYZ
0123456789 0123456789

abcdefghijklmnopqrstuvwxyz
ABCDEFGHIJKLMNOPQRSTUVWXYZ
ABCDEFGHIJKLMNOPQRSTUVWXYZ
0123456789 0123456789

abcdefghijklmnopqrstuvwxyz
ABCDEFGHIJKLMNOPQRSTUVWXYZ
ABCDEFGHIJKLMNOPQRSTUVWXYZ
0123456789 0123456789

het doek voor het eerst in Museum Boijmans van Beuningen. Het is 76,5 centimeter breed en 67 centimeter hoog. Ik was diep onder de indruk. Deze vrouw, zorgvuldig opgeborgen in haar serene cocon, haar borsten in duistere draperie, haar rechterhand elegant om de te zalven penis, verzamelde alle vrouwelijkheid in een blik die mij volledig in beslag nam. Alles aan haar was rond en zacht en wijs; haar omgeving bizar, grillig. Haar frêle aanwezigheid spinde mij in een roes die ik jarenlang op commando kon oproepen. Ik interpreteerde het schilderij als één van de blauwdrukken van de voor mij liggende tijd.

01.05 Toen ik het doek decennia later terugzag viel mij de zelfbewuste, bijna hautaine blik op, het vreemde platgeslagen linkeroor, de al te nadrukkelijke ovaal van het gelaat en de vlakke coulissen die de achtergrond vormden. De wijze waarop de schilder haar horen had gedrapeerd, haar hand op de zolfbus had gelegd en het licht op de erogene driehoek van haar hals liet spelen, bekoorden opnieuw.

VERLEIDING
02.01 Rondom mij: water, rietkragen, bomen, insekten en de verschrikkelijke meeuwen die de avonden vol krijsen telkens wanneer ze zich van de broedkolonie losmaken. Ik bevind mij in vrijwillige ballingschap. Het huis verborgen achter een muur van groen, vanaf de dijk onzichtbaar, voorzien van afzuigkap, centrale verwarming, beeldscherm, telefoon en een reu die me de hele dag achterna loopt omdat dat zijn kansen op overleving waarborgt.
02.02 In dit stiltegebied verzamelden zich de hier genoteerde aantekeningen. In afgemeten pretentie schetsen zij de actuele,

haast puberale worsteling van de 'Dierentuin der Dierentuinen': het museum voor hedendaagse beeldende kunst. Dit museum, dat zich voorheen manifesteerde als een zwijgende adolescent (een pokdalige nerd, voorbestemd tot een cultureel pastoraat waar perioden van diepe wijsheid worden afgewisseld met perioden van heftige masturbatie), lijkt zich nu te maken voor een nieuwe maatschappelijke opdracht: de verleiding.

NATURA ARTIS MAGISTRA
03.01 Dierentuinen en musea hebben zich volgens vrijwel identieke lijnen ontwikkeld. Vanaf het moment dat naties zeeën bevoeren, namen zij trofeeën als bewijsvoering mee naar huis. Dat leverde rariteitenkabinetten op als *Wunderkammer* (de latere volkenkundige musea), botanische tuinen, naturaliënkabinetten en menagerieën. Menagerieën, dierentuinen bestonden nog niet, waren die delen van de paleistuin waar de exoten werden ondergebracht en in kleine kring geëxposeerd. De dierentuin die het meest aan een menagerie herinnert treft men in Wenen aan: Tiergarten Schönbrunn uit 1752.
03.02 Diervriendelijk waren de men[...] bedoeld om de status van de eigenar[...] te waarderen; het welzijn van de dier[...] geschikt.
03.03 De in de 18e eeuw opkomende [...] snel in de gaten dat er aan exoten te [...] dig exploiteerden zij 'rondreizende m[...] cussen waar de exoten aan het publie[...] enkel dieren, ook dwergen (boer Lol[...]

Q.S.SerafijnMU
SEUMALSPRETP
ARK!Aantekenin
go437Proba0001
Uitgeverij3005

Design	This Studio
Project	Kristen Whittle
Category	Identity / stationery
Date	2005

A clean, crisp, understated identity and stationery range for an architect based in Australia. The identity is formed from the architect's initials which appear in thin hairline characters. Heavier curved radii are placed at the intersections of the letters, giving greater strength and stability to their forms. In this way the characters resemble an architect's cross-section drawings. The stationery is printed simply in a dark warm grey; the back of each item is printed full-bleed in the same dark grey with a mirror image of the typography reversed out in white.

Design	This Studio
Project	Martyn James Brooks
Category	Mailer / poster
Date	2005

This promotional poster for the London-based photographer is printed on a very thin uncoated stock, which makes it very delicate. The typography, which is set in a clean sans-serif font, is rendered as a series of thin vertical lines, allowing very large type to appear faint and not detract from the black-and-white photograph which is just visible through the translucent paper. The same typography is printed over the image, although the thin lines become lost in the density of the photograph.

Design   Spin
Project   Visuell 25 – Deutsche Bank
Category   Magazine
Date   2005

Though produced as a magazine, *Visuell* boasts a page
count in excess of 300 and takes on the proportions of a
book or catalogue. Published in two versions, English and
German, and printed predominantly in four colour
complemented with metallic silver and fluorescent pink,
it serves as a vehicle for Deutsche Bank's extensive art-
world interests. The designers keep the typography fresh
and exciting throughout by playing with scale, setting text
in diagonally aligned columns and a whole host of other
experiments.

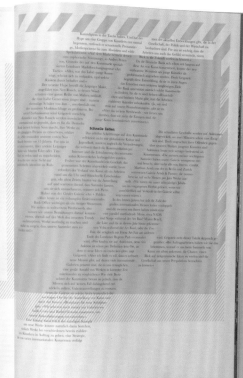
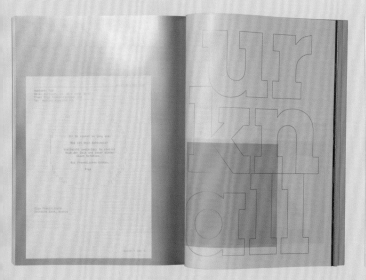

type as image

As a backlash against the clean, razor-sharp purity of digitally generated typography, designers are looking to traditional and vernacular sources to produce typography with a more illustrative and hand-drawn aesthetic.

The pleasure of noise

Cities can be exhilarating, demanding and noisy. This sensory cacophony can be alluring and commercial enterprises recognize this. The variety and scale of letters attached to buildings, hoardings and vehicles can transform them into abstract images which invite discretion to be abandoned.

The function of these images is to be as noisy as possible, their primary purpose being to attract at all costs. Advertising, graffiti, fly-posters, stickers, temporary signs and notices, and shop fascias are an integral part of urban living and working. And all are noisy. The printed media we read – newspapers, magazines – and websites we visit are also littered with type as image, screaming, laughing, or crying at us. The arbitrary nature and variety of this material can be both entertaining and offensive, depending on your view of unsolicited 'information'. But what it all has in common is that it cannot be avoided.

Much of this typographic matter on our streets will have been produced by non-designers, some by vandals, and some (usually quite a small percentage) by professional typographers. City streets are a valuable and effective medium through which to disseminate information indiscriminately. Meanwhile, the relatively high costs incurred using commercial print ensures a level of control of type and images for mass-circulation material. These noise levels can be manipulated, the volume turned up or down, depending upon the interests of the editor or proprietor of the publication. But city streets are far more difficult to control and the unpredictability of location and the circumstances of the viewer require that the volume remain at a constant high. In typographic terms such material is 'noise'. As such, typographic imagery is particularly effective at attracting attention.

In older, more neglected districts of a large town or city can be found the remnants of businesses from previous generations, providing rich clues of previous sociopolitical change. The majority of urban typographic imagery will have been the result of confidence in the future: a good idea, something new, exciting and worth shouting about.

The professional typographer's work will be most easily recognized in the street signage, locational identity signs, and situational, ad hoc information that every town and city requires if it is to function in an orderly manner. There will also be rule-governed brandings: corporate logos, names and associated livery. Other signs might be bespoke: one-off signs on buildings, vehicles and sale offers. All of these will carry the mark of the typographer.

And yet, it is the amateur's hand-rendered notice or sign which so often catches our attention because it is (intentionally or not) different from those designed by the professional. Such material appears to be out of control (in both appearance and placement) because it lacks the 'sophistication' ('predictability'?) we have come to expect of the carefully maintained corporate image or message in the public domain. This can be either alarming or charming. However, to be effective, information must always attract for the right reason and certainly, in the urban commercial environment, the public are highly attuned to the way information is relayed to them. An informal price sign made in haste for a market stall will not be perceived as indicating lack of concern by the stallholder for the quality of his fresh fruit; quite the opposite. The information and the images it carries are immediate and impermanent, both qualities being appropriate for the selling of fresh food. However, if a permanent (formal) sign, displaying the stallholder's name, for example, is hurriedly and ineptly done, its informality will be perceived to be inappropriate. When typography is 'wrong' it is obvious to all and there can be no clearer signal of indolence and deceitfulness. But such material can also offer an honest innocence that is alluring in its careful, if inept, execution. There is a fine line between beauty and ugliness, between appropriate and inappropriate. There is ample evidence on the following pages of typographers using aspects of the informal detritus of the streets: signs and symbols that signal messages in crude shorthand to those 'in the know'. The image created, and the media emphatically displayed, all suggest a renewed interest in the power of the hand-made, the personal and idiosyncratic message.

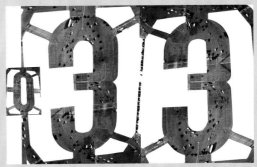

In sharp contrast, the long-established department store generally makes every effort to present a consistent and highly predictable, formal appearance on the high street (even if it prides itself on warm and friendly [informal] service). A less formal method of conveying information can still be initiated for short-term events such as a sale, but this material must be disposed of the moment the event is over, so as to enable the formal appearance of the business to be resumed.

People appreciate the effort involved (if not the process) in the production of notices and signs. Something that requires time to plan and then paint or carve, print or build, will generally be considered more formal because it has gone through a discernible process of design, making and/or manufacture and installation, and is already clearly intended to be in place for a considerable time. The materials chosen are very important in reflecting this. They contribute to its value which, in turn, projects value upon its 'owner'. Letterforms bought 'off the shelf' and fixed, DIY style, by the individual business entrepreneur, and even by authoritative organizations, give rise to classic disasters: 'M' and 'W' mixed up, various characters upside down and, more commonly, poor spacing. Off-the-shelf letters lack the author's voice and, therefore, fail to convey a sense of authenticity or ownership. The lack of integrity and permanence is palpable in such instances. However, the blandness of image so regularly considered to be the appropriate typographic response in corporate society is often no better.

This has not always been the case. Before letters could be so easily and cheaply manufactured, examples of lettering and signing offered a sense of both time and place. This material was a rich source of study for those keen to promote the study of letterforms. The writings of Alan Bartram, Nicolette Gray, James Mosley and, more recently, Phil Baines and Catherine Dixon provide robust support for maintaining highly individual typographic imagery and lettering on buildings and in all public places.

A degree of informality on the high street is not so much tolerated as cherished. Informality is necessary in order to preserve a town's or city's identity. It is, of course, necessary for the high street to be formal to a degree because it is a public domain, but it is also a place of theatre (*theatrum mundi*), where people play out their public roles and where commercial businesses and entertainment venues present an indeterminate sort of dynamism, always noisily, which we accept with a mixture of irony, occasional disbelief and, perhaps, good humour. When these characteristics are combined, the attraction is inevitable! Sagmeister (above left) is the master of such contradictory combinations, the results of which not only attract but remain in the mind long after the page has been turned. Such qualities are, perhaps, inevitably disturbing, but surely preferable to the constant whimper of polite 'good taste'.

The act of 'play' is also attractive, and the offer to participate a beguiling compliment. By playing with convention, the cover design of a women's fashion or lifestyle magazine (for example, by Grandpeople, far left) can provide the opportunity to remind us of the dross we cannot avoid seeing every day. The letterforms, determinedly unsophisticated and physically attached to the 'cover model', can be deciphered, eventually, this participation committing the reader to the message.

Advertising provides a similarly noisy mix and remains a prime provider of type as image. Clichés, puns, aphorisms, slogans, truisms and platitudes: these are typical linguistic forms that we associate with advertising. Their scale is in direct contrast to the smallness of commonplace and often vapid or trite typographic images.[1] The noise level is deafening, the mix of bravado and silliness astonishing.

Type on the streets, whether permanent or transient, is unsolicited but there is little chance of avoiding it. In fact, it will have been positioned to ensure that you cannot avoid seeing it. But, over time, a combination of selective cognizance, plus the effects of pollution and weather, will generally weaken the influence of even the worst kind of typographic noise.

In fact, it is a very good idea to consider how any designed item will look in 10, 20 or 100 years' time. (Not a problem the advertising industry generally needs to consider.) 'Decay is the most powerful medium for the improvement of cities… Decay, not architects, adds the last touches, blackens and peels the stone, applies lichens and cracks, softens the edges, elaborates elaboration, and the hand of man works even better than the forces of nature.'[2] Similarly, a scuffed, well-thumbed book with scribbled notes in the margins and turned-down page corners is the unavoidable consequence of a well-used and truly useful document.

1 Joan Gibbons, 'Beyond Banality', *TypoGraphic* 65, International Society of Typographic Designers, 2006.

2 Barbara Jones, writing about the photographs recording 'typographic detritus or chance art' on the streets of London by Herbert Spencer in 1963. *Typographica*, n.s. 8.

Design	Grandpeople
Project	Random System Festival
Category	Poster
Date	2004

Produced for the Random System music festival in Oslo, the poster's headline typography was created from modelling clay and shot as part of a still-life set-up. All secondary information is set in white panels at the top of the poster in more conventional typographic style.

Design	Grandpeople
Project	Safe as Milk Festival #7
Category	Poster
Date	2005

Safe as Milk is an annual music festival held in Norway. For the promotional material and poster for the seventh festival, the designers created the branding and all the headline typography from a thick gluey paint, which has been photographed in such a way as to retain its full three-dimensional quality. The seemingly casual feel of the typography gives the poster a vernacular air. As a contrast to this hand-drawn quality, all the other elements on the poster are computer-generated.

Design	Grandpeople
Project	Collecting Flowers
Category	Poster / folder
Date	2006

This poster/folder for Oslo Arkitektforening, a Norwegian architectural organization, uses found pieces of litter for its raw typographic foundations. Each crushed tin can or offcut of wood is treated as a delicate pressed flower to reflect the title. Parts of these found objects have been cut out to aid the legibility of the letterform. All the same, at first sight the litter is not instantly recognizable as a typeface. The secondary headline is a stylized hairline font, with a strong Art Deco flavour.

Design	Grandpeople
Project	Random Cube
Category	Poster / visual profile
Date	2005

When the 2005 Random System Festival moved to a new venue called Black Box in Oslo, the event changed its name to Random Cube to reflect its new location. With reduced printing budgets, the poster was produced in a single colour printed on different-coloured stocks: yellow, pink, orange and white. The typography is again hand-drawn, with drawn drips of 'wet' paint. The legibility decreases the further down the poster you look.

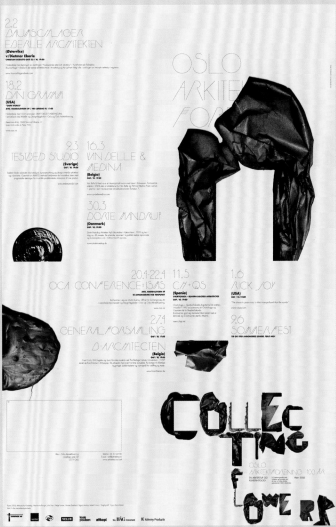

Design	Grandpeople
Project	Hat Hat Hat
Category	Poster / visual profile
Date	2005

The typography on this poster becomes one with the illustration, forming an almost symmetrical illustration. The psychedelia-inspired illustration is printed in a graduated colour blend from black to purple, with the root-like typography branching out at the top.

Image
74

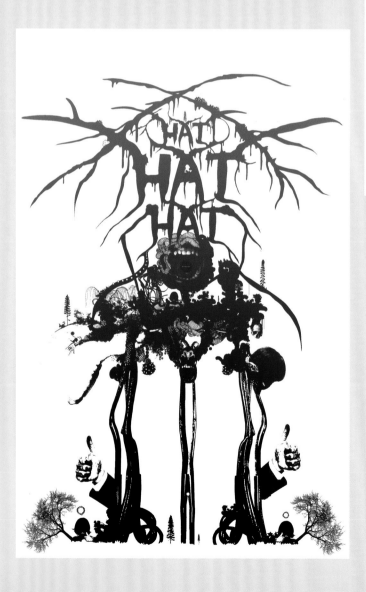

Design	Grandpeople
Project	XXVII
Category	Book design / visual profile
Date	2005

A hand-painted large-format poster is the starting point for the cover of an exhibition catalogue for the Bergen National Academy of the Arts in Norway. The title 'XXVII', derived from the fact that 27 students took part in the show, was hand-painted onto the large sheet of brown paper and then held up and photographed in a studio environment. The other typographic elements were then digitally overprinted in the designers' own font Maria, which is a decorative single line-thickness face that uses a traditional Scandinavian cross-stitch aesthetic.

Design	Grandpeople
Project	Utflukt
Category	Magazine cover
Date	2005

The designers were commissioned to design the front cover of *Utflukt*, a Norwegian cultural magazine. The theme for the issue was 'anti-design'. The magazine's masthead runs across the top in a white banner (not shown here). The designers wanted to play with the convention of a head shot on the cover, as used on every women's fashion magazine in the world. However, in this version the head shot becomes covered in blobby letterforms held and stuck onto the face of the cover star (a member of Grandpeople). These letterforms make up the title – 'Anti-design'.

Design	Grandpeople
Project	BMB – Brättne Skyline
Category	CD cover
Date	2005

For the fifth album by BMB (Bergen Madolin Band), a mix of geometric shapes are used to form the titles of the tracks. Black-and-white halftone images are used on some of these bold characters in contrast to others in heavy solid black. The density of the characters is balanced by the introduction of some hairline linear letterforms. All other information on the CD is set in a more conventional serif font.

Design	Kim Hiorthøy
Project	Hidros 3
Category	Record sleeve
Date	2005

The typography for this cover is formed from a conventional bold condensed sans-serif font. However, it has been personalized by the addition of some hand-drawn flames and a heavy black drop shadow. Each letterform is hand-positioned, giving the sleeve a cut-and-paste quality.

Design	Kim Hiorthøy
Project	David Grubbs: A Guess at the Riddle
Category	Record sleeve
Date	2005

This predominantly typographic cover again uses a very bold slab-serif font as its foundations. The letterforms have been redrawn and given the freedom to bleed into each other as well as to form partial shadows and become one with the illustrated background.

Design	Kim Hiorthøy
Project	DJ Sunshine
Category	Poster
Date	2005

This poster has the aesthetic of a home-made punk flyer from the mid-1970s: coarse halftone image, badly drawn and stencil lettering. However, it is given a contemporary twist in the style of the lettering adopted for 'Benji B' and 'DJ Sunshine', which are formed from softer, more organic shapes, in marked contrast to the rest of the rather spikier typography.

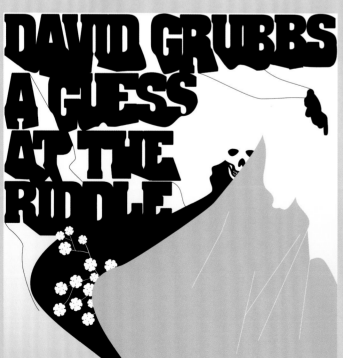

Design	Kim Hiorthøy
Project	Lars Horntveth: The Joker EP
Category	Record sleeve
Date	2005

The soft organic letterforms fluidly move around the square white canvas in a freeform manner. Painted by hand with brush strokes clearly visible, the autumnal palette of colours helps to differentiate each piece of information on the sleeve.

Design	Grandpeople
Project	Alexander Rishaug: Rooftop Camping
Category	3-inch CD sleeve design
Date	2004

Avoiding the clichés of sleeve design for experimental electronic music, the designers created something light-hearted and playful. In an allusion to psychedelic posters of the Sixties, the soft letterforms collide and merge with each other. The colour palette of pinks, bright greens and yellows gives the sleeve a contemporary Japanese cartoon feel.

Design	Kim Hiorthøy
Project	Open Day
Category	Poster
Date	2005

This poster for an event during London Fashion Week constructs an unstable tower of hairline typography from letters of different colours. The composition uses the full height of the poster to maximize the effect, with the soft hand-drawn letters precariously balanced on top of one another.

Design	Grandpeople
Project	BIFF Utstillingen
Category	Folder
Date	2004

Produced for a video art exhibition at the Bergen International Film Festival (BIFF) in Sweden, the treatment of the title gives a sense of projected film and light. The clean hard edges of the BIFF title are softened through the use of overprinted graduated tints. Strange blobby typographic shapes appear in outlined form in the background and are used elsewhere on the folder.

Design	Stiletto
Project	Stiletto identity
Category	Visual identity
Date	2004

This New York-based graphic design agency have created their own font to help unify all aspects of their printed stationery range. The letterforms have an irregular line thickness and look as if they have been generated from lines of masking tape stuck down to form a squared font.

Image
78

Design	Non–Format
Project	Pompei
Category	Catalogue
Date	2005

Programme and catalogue for the 37th International Theatre Festival at the Venice Biennale. The two are bound together with a rubber band which is held in place by die-cut indents at the top and bottom of the books. A headline font with an open circular linear form was specially created for the project. The 'a', 'b', 'd', 'g', 'i', 'o', 'p' and 'q' feature solid black infilled circles, with fragments of decaying flowers and soil around them.

Design	Studio Thomson
Project	Preen invitation
Category	Mailer
Date	2005

This card, which unfolds in a star-shaped manner, has an axometric grid printed over its surface. The designers redrew the logo for this London fashion event by hand using the triangular shapes found in the graph lines.

Design	Exposure
Project	The Advertising Is Dead!
Category	Poster
Date	2005

Produced in a self-published run of 150, this poster comments on the changing nature of mass communication and its move away from traditional mediums to more organic ones. The text is set in a bold sans-serif headline font with two treatments – one bold and traditional, the other loosely handcrafted and organic.

THE ADVERTISING IS DEAD! LONG LIVE THE ADVERTISING!

Design	Exposure
Project	Tom Binns
Category	Postcards
Date	2006

A series of postcards were produced to introduce the new brand identity work for LA-based jeweller Tom Binns. The jeweller has the image of a renegade and he wanted this attitude to come through in the identity. In keeping with this, his name is applied using a strong bold neon type treatment over existing couture logos. The latter have been hastily scribbled out in black pen, leaving just enough visible, however, for the cancelled brand names to be legible underneath.

Design	Exposure
Project	Organic Type
Category	Poster
Date	2006

A sequence of words and phrases are seemingly randomly featured on this poster. Printed in various pastel shades, the type is loosely hand-drawn to echo various half-remembered headline fonts. The poster almost looks like a teenager's school book doodled over with slogans.

Design	3 Deep Design
Project	Poster Magazine: Issue 08
Category	Magazine design
Date	2005

Founded in 2001, *Poster Magazine* has established itself at the forefront of contemporary fashion. Each issue of the quarterly publication features a new headline font, which is also used for the cover. As a result, each issue has a unique look. Issue 08 developed a linear semi-joined-up font which has an intriguing flowery quality.

Design	3 Deep Design
Project	Poster Magazine: Issue 09
Category	Magazine design
Date	2005

Issue 09 of this quarterly publication replaces the standard formal typographic headlines with loose handwriting scrawled across the page in thick marker pen. The out-of-control lettering looks as if it was done while blindfolded and using the wrong hand.

Image

82

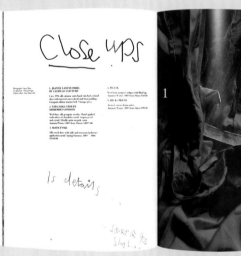

Design   Wladimir Marnich
Project   Chic
Category   Magazine design
Date   2005

Chic is a Spanish glossy women's monthly. The art director has used a bold curvaceous serif font to create large playful graphic opening spreads for features, sometimes bleeding the letterforms off the page to create semi-abstract shapes and at other times simply setting the title as large as possible while retaining legibility.

Design	Exposure
Project	Organic Type
Category	Poster
Date	2006

A series of loosely hand-drawn stylized speech bubbles, printed onto a canvas poster, contain a variety of different typographic treatments emulating typical corporate logos.

Design	Kim Hiorthøy
Project	Factory Anagrams
Category	Visual identity
Date	2005

This identity for Factory Films in London uses vernacular type of the sort often seen in dusty old cafés, where letters can be pushed into the grooves on pieces of plastic backing board. Here a series of anagrams are formed from the company's name. The characters are misaligned and sometimes almost falling off the page. This sense of play and humour is not usually associated with corporate-identity work.

Design	A2/SW/HK
Project	Typo-Graphic Exp.
Category	Poster
Date	2006

This poster, produced to advertise and promote a four-day typographic workshop given by the designers, combines clean serifed typography with gritty imagery. The latter illustrates one of the key themes of the workshop, 'Typography by Hand', with elegant simplicity. The very coarse halftone of a hand grasping two marker pens held together to form the letter 'T' creates a striking graphic image.

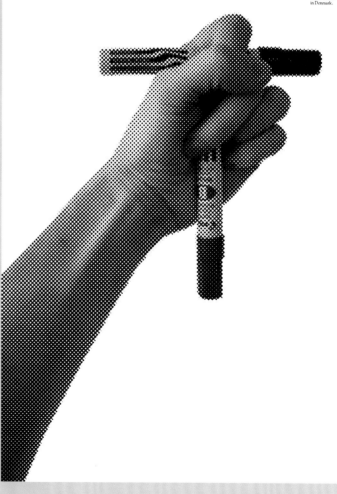

TYPO-GRAPHIC EXP.

A four day workshop exploring: *Typography by hand – National and International identity – Poster design & the creation of Bespoke typefaces.*

During the workshop there will be a portfolio review and each student is asked to bring a selection of recent projects to discuss.

Henrik Kubel graduated from Denmarks Design School in 1997 and from the Royal College of Art's Communication Art & Design Department in London in 2000. Upon graduation Kubel and fellow graduate Scott Williams formed the creative Design & Typography studio A2/SW/HK based in London. The duo specialise in design for print (mostly books and artist catalogues), development of bespoke typography and exhibition design. A2/SW/HK have worked for clients such as British Council, V&A Museum, Phaidon, Royal Mail, Tate Britain, Tate Modern, Tate Liverpool, Hayward Gallery, Vogue UK, Afterall journal, Aveny-T, 1508, Noerrebros Bryghus, Kolding Kommune and Kunstuff Magazine.

Most recently they designed the cover of the American version of Zadie Smiths 'On Beauty' for Penguin Press in New York and have just completed the design of the annual Turner Prize exhibition at Tate Britain. The studio are currently working on a photography book for Phaidon, an identity programme including corporate typefaces for an architectural practice in Newcastle, two artist books, a book on contemporary furniture for V&A Museum, a catalogue for Siemens Arts programme UK & a signage project for Kolding Council in Denmark.

Design	A2/SW/HK
Project	Typography Workshop
Category	Posters
Date	2000–ongoing

A series of 40-plus posters designed for a typography workshop given by the designers at Buckinghamshire Chilterns University College. Each poster has the same basic format: printed in black and white, landscape in orientation and with an information strip running across the top edge. The illustration area is usually filled with a hand-drawn typographic idea. The posters therefore convey a sense of immediacy – the idea is what counts, not the execution.

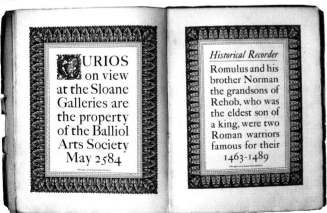

Design	Stiletto
Project	As Four
Category	Visual identity / printed matter
Date	2005

The calligraphy in this identity has an arabesque-like fluidity to it. The uppercase 'A' and the numeral '4' have similar visual qualities which allow them to morph together. The supporting typography is set in a strong bold all-caps sans serif to give a clean modern edge to the identity.

Image
86

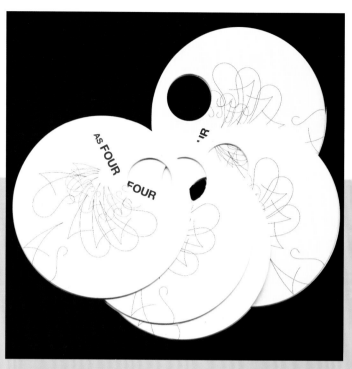

Design	Al Mohtaraf Design
Project	Modern
Category	Type design / poster
Date	2005

Poster promoting Modern, an original display typeface, from the collection of Arabic fonts designed by Al Mohtaraf. The geometric clean-cut form of the font is illustrated by the large letterforms that extend across the whole poster. Construction lines are included on the poster, showing the development and structure of the characters.

Design	Al Mohtaraf Design
Project	Midan
Category	Type design / poster
Date	2006

Poster promoting Midan, a humanist Arabic typeface designed by Kameel Hawa and based on open counters and a strong horizontal stress suitable for setting long passages of text. This typeface won the Hermann Zapf choice award at the first Linotype Arabic competition, 2006, in addition to the second prize in the text category. The poster illustrates the font in various sizes of text and headline setting.

Design	Al Mohtaraf Design
Project	Naktub Isman
Category	Booklet
Date	2005

This booklet presents a collection of names, some of which use traditional calligraphic styles while others explore innovative approaches to expression and representation. 'Milh', meaning salt, is one clear example of an illustrative use of calligraphy, used as a title for an article in a magazine. The calligraphy is on the pivotal point between illustration and typography. Arabic fonts offer far greater levels of flexibility, allowing the calligrapher/designer to push the form of the letters further than would be acceptable in a roman font.

Design   Oded Ezer
Project   Various typographic projects
Category   Posters
Date   2004

Ezer's typographic work ranges from expressive calligraphy to hardworking practical fonts. Shown here are three of his more expressive Hebrew faces which play with extreme thicknesses and thinnesses to create fonts of a truly modern nature.

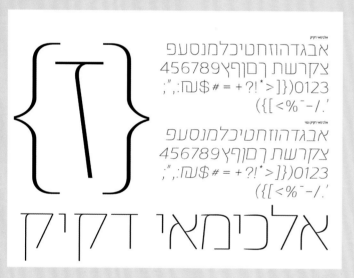

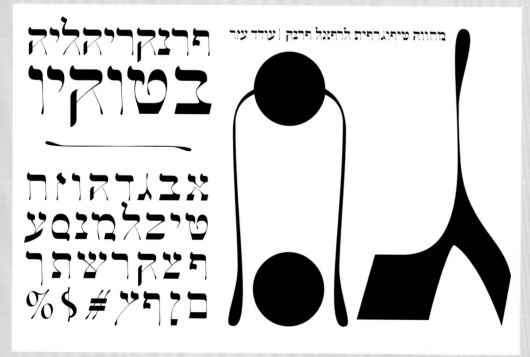

Design	Peter Anderson / Interfield Design
Project	Alive + Well Health Centre
Category	Visual identity
Date	2005

The clean typographic listing of services on offer at this health centre is organized like an eyesight test, with key words printed in a range of sizes, starting very small and increasing in size down the page. The designer also produced a series of more freeform typographic doodles for use around the clinic.

Design	Peter Anderson / Interfield Design
Project	Welsh Tourist Board
Category	Advertising
Date	2005

The wild mane of a galloping horse shapes the animated, flowing typography, which is set in various point sizes and swirls from the horse's neck.

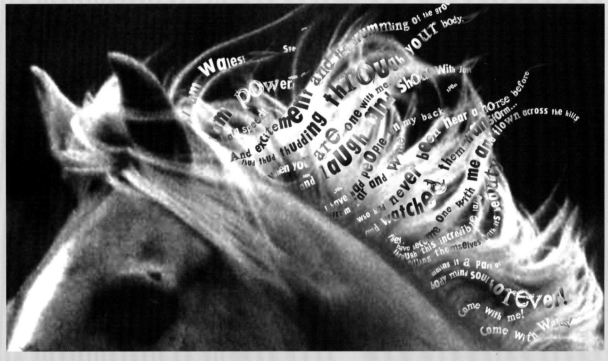

Design	Peter Anderson / Interfield Design
Project	Cayenne
Category	Restaurant graphics
Date	2005

A series of quotes are displayed throughout this fashionable restaurant. The playful typography and rich palette of colours are a key element in its interior design. The pieces range from neon signs to printed typography and have varying degrees of legibility.

Image
90

Design	Peter Anderson / Interfield Design
Project	Rain City Restaurant
Category	Visual identity
Date	2005

A series of loose hand-drawn artworks were created for this vibrant Belfast restaurant. The energetic typography, although printed in single colours, has a real energy, which helps to create a buzzy ambience.

Design	FL@33
Project	SCSI font
Category	Magazine layouts
Date	2004

Illustration and 'SCSI' typeface design for a *Creative Review* feature on Rick Poynor's book *Communicate: Independent British Graphic Design since the Sixties.* The letter shapes are formed from now-obsolete SCSI computer connection cables. The lettering has a handwritten quality which is at odds with the digital source material.

Design	Projekttriangle
Project	Future Hair
Category	Visual identity / folder
Date	2005

Printed in black and fluorescent pink, this visual identity uses a custom-designed typeface with a thin rounded line. Black-and-white photographs of a model are overprinted with strands of hair that snake across the imagery in fluorescent pink or reversed out in white. The font joins up the letters to create a curvaceous, flowing logo.

Design	A2/SW/HK
Project	Zadie Smith: On Beauty
Category	Book cover
Date	2005

The typography on this jacket epitomizes the novel's announced subject matter. The headline font was specially created for the project and has its roots in a version of Bodoni. However, the designers have simplified the form and also added some flamboyant swirls. The lettering is foil-blocked in red onto the cream cover paper. The type line work is also embossed, which gives the jacket a three-dimensional quality.

Image
92

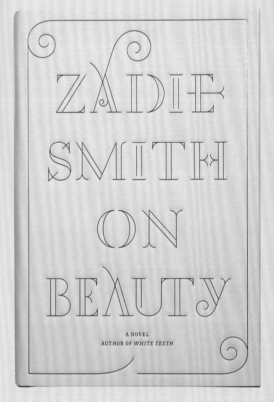

Design	BB/Saunders
Project	Tabooboo
Category	Visual identity / printed matter
Date	2006

The identity for this upmarket sex shop uses a curvaceous font that makes the most of the 'o's in the name. The printed material features thin line drawings of forbidden fruits and oozing honey. All other typography is set in VAG Rounded, which bears a strong similarity to that of the identity and is printed as an outline version, which ties in with the illustration style.

Design	Non-Format
Project	Norway 1905–2005
Category	Poster
Date	2005

Produced for the Royal Norwegian Embassy in London, this poster features the contours of Norway printed in gold and formed from a series of small pictograms of activities associated with the country. The headline font is constructed from a silhouette of a cheese slice: by combining the handle and half-oval form of the slice it is possible to construct all the required lettershapes.

Design	Studio 3005
Project	D-Toren
Category	Poster
Date	2005

D-Toren (D-Tower in English) is a sculpture/installation-based art project commissioned by the city of Doetinchem in the Netherlands which maps the emotions of its inhabitants. The project was conceived by the artist Q.S. Serafijn and Lars Spuybroek/NOX-Architekten. This poster combines elements from a questionnaire with CAD renderings of the sculpture. The layered typography relates to the four emotional states – 'HAPPINESS', 'LOVE', 'FEAR' and 'HATE' – mapped by the D-Tower.

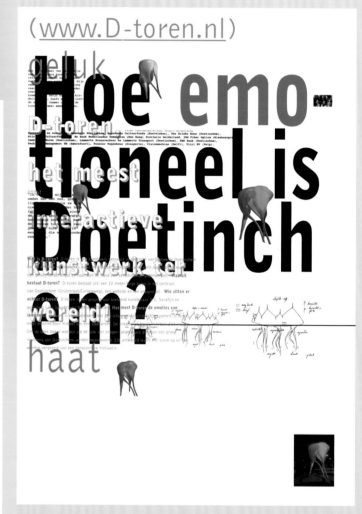

Design	Kim Hiorthøy
Project	Jaga Jazzist: The Stix
Category	Record sleeve
Date	2005

Design	Kim Hiorthøy
Project	Various Artists: STS
Category	Record sleeve
Date	2005

Design	Kim Hiorthøy
Project	Jaga Jazzist: A Livingroom Hush
Category	Record sleeve
Date	2005

These three record sleeves produced for Ninja Tune/
Smalltown Supersound Records feature a more heavily
computer-rendered CAD approach than is usually
associated with the designer, and combine montaged gritty
photography with slick hard typographic edges.

Design   Research Studios
Project   Interact 1
Category   Poster
Date   2004

'Interact 1' was an exhibition exploring the future of visual
communication, bringing together some of the UK's leading
design professionals and students. A series of six posters
were produced showcasing work by three students and
their professional designer-mentors and using themes
generated from the exhibition. Reproduced here are the
posters by Neville Brody and Ben Reece.

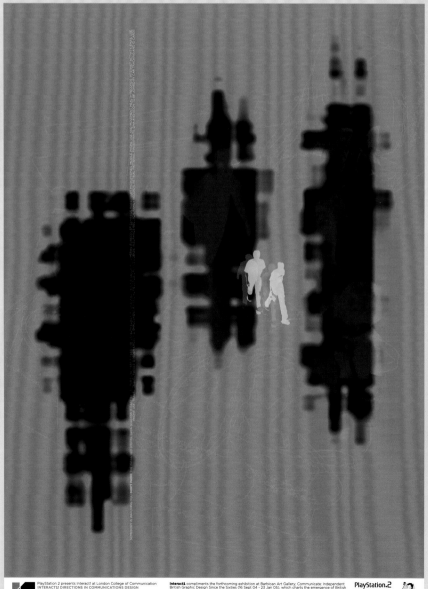

Design	Research Studios
Project	Exberliner
Category	Invite / flyer
Date	2004

Research Studios designed the masthead and various covers, as well as contributing ideas to inside layouts, for *Exberliner*, the English-language Berlin newspaper. Shown here are two colour variations for a second-birthday party invite/flyer. The large number '2' is generated from a series of overlapping diagonal lines.

Design	Research Studios
Project	Computer Arts Projects
Category	Magazine cover
Date	2005

Research Studios regularly contributes cover designs and section spreads to the magazine *Computer Arts Projects*. Shown here is a design concept for the cover of an issue about typography. The morphic letterforms feature translucent layers that build up to create dense forms similar to the gradients shown on contour maps of mountainous regions.

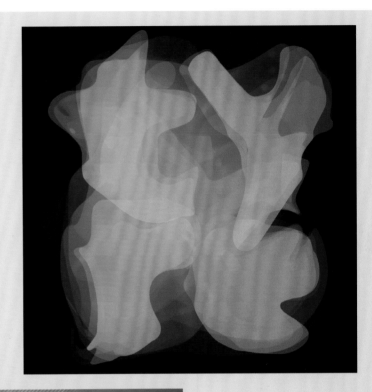

Design	Studio Philippe Apeloig
Project	Günter Grass
Category	Poster
Date	2005

This poster combines imagery and typography into a single entity set against a white background. The headline type is cut and cropped to fill the rectangular format of the poster, which gives the treatment a playful quality. The sepia-coloured portrait is also tightly cropped, with elements placed within the letterforms. Years from 1900 to 1999 are printed very small in red, set on a diagonal grid which runs over the entire surface of the poster.

Design	Studio Philippe Apeloig
Project	Demain La Bibliothèque
Category	Poster
Date	2006

Produced for an exhibition held by the Association des Bibliothécaires Français in Paris, this poster combines two levels of information. A series of different-sized oval shapes are combined with rectangles to form an abstracted alphabet, printed white out of a brown background. A smaller translucent purple rectangle is then overprinted containing full details of the exhibition set in a more conventional typeface.

Design	Saturday
Project	J. Lindeberg Future Sports Golf / Ski
Category	Visual identity / packaging / brochure
Date	2005

A dot-matrix font is used for this sports-range identity to create a dynamic, evolving branding system. Dot-matrix typefaces often make an appearance at sporting events on large electronic displays that give timings, results and other information. Here, the designers have combined this characteristic typographic styling with a palette of vibrant colours, at odds with those normally associated with golf, in order to give the identity a fresh modern twist. The dot structure used on the font itself is repeated over large areas of the printed surface.

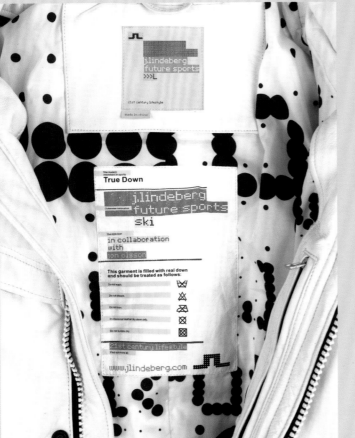

Design	FL@33
Project	Dalai Lama Speech
Category	Poster
Date	2003

For an exhibition called 'Public Address System' 40 designers were asked to create a poster interpreting a public speech of their choice, ranging from great political addresses to song lyrics. The exhibition was organized by the Henry Peacock Gallery and *Grafik* magazine. This one interprets a speech by the Dalai Lama to the European Parliament in October 2001. The text is broken into three sections sculpted into the shape of three warring figures wielding rocks, swords and guns. Key sentences are highlighted in fluorescent orange.

Design	FL@33
Project	ASCII Animation
Category	Animation
Date	2003

The designers were commissioned by Alsop Architects in London to design an installation for an exhibition called 'A&M (Department Stores of Proper Behaviour)' at the Valencia Biennale. The project was organized by Will Alsop and Bruce McLean. The designer's installation was called 'Reading Department' and featured ASCII-based animated sequences of a close-up of an eye which appears to be reading lines of imagined text. The sequences were shown on television screens built into confessional boxes.

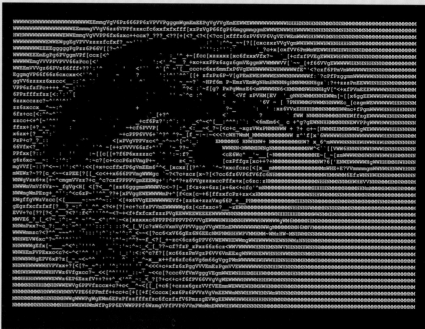

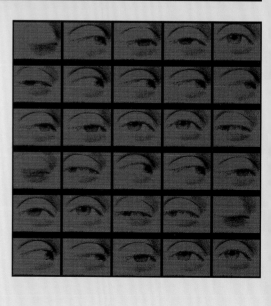

Design	Exposure
Project	Tom Binns: AMO
Category	Postcard
Date	2005

This postcard for the LA-based jeweller Tom Binns creates the letters 'AMO' from the negative spaces of the illustration. The latter consists of hundreds of small black-and-white reproductions of pieces of the designer's jewellery which have been carefully arranged to form the outline of the sans-serif letterforms. As such, there is no need for the letters to be printed white out of the illustration.

Design	Alias
Project	Star Culture
Category	Book
Date	2004

Comprising interviews from *Dazed & Confused* magazine, this book has cover and section divider pages that use moiré effects to create optically challenging titles. The text is hidden inside the overlapping dot structures generated by the four-colour print process. The increased size and coarse quality of these pages could also relate to the idea that these are 'reprints' – not the original interviews, but a second generation.

Design	Work By Lunch
Project	Overload
Category	Magazine illustration
Date	2006

This typographic illustration was created for *Slash* magazine. The letterforms are created from densely packed pictograms of bottles. As if to illustrate the effects of too much drink, they start to disintegrate at the baseline.

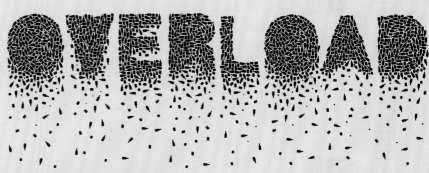

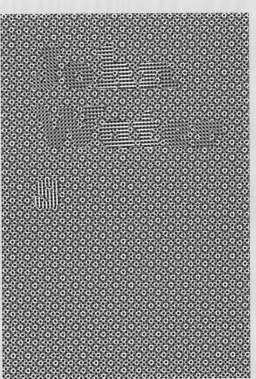

Design	NB Studios
Project	Totalcontent
Category	Visual identity / stationery
Date	2006

A playful typographic composition was created using woodblock letters and then printed on the back of various stationery items. It was adopted as the company's identity even though it doesn't actually give its name – the latter is simply printed in a clean sans serif along with the necessary address information.

Design	Exposure
Project	Dr Martens Magic
Category	Invite
Date	2006

An invitation to a trade show is mailed out in a black rubber vacuum-packed bag, which highlights the strange three-dimensional shape within. When the bag is opened, the invite itself is found to consist of a bright yellow bootlace wrapped around a typographic card. Black and yellow are the colours most commonly associated with Dr Martens, especially the bright yellow lace. The bold sans-serif type is bound by the lace.

Design	FL@33
Project	Pencil Sculpture Illustration Series
Category	Magazine cover
Date	2002

Commissioned by *Creative Review*, the brief for this piece was to illustrate '40 years of D&AD'. The designers created an illustration from a stack of yellow pencils, a symbol closely associated with the D&AD, laid at a 45-degree angle. The '40' is given a dynamic drop shadow by the pencil ends.

Design	FL@33
Project	Street Font
Category	Illustration
Date	2004

This piece proves that, with a bit of digital manipulation, typographic forms can be found anywhere and everywhere. After comping together various aerial photographs of road junctions and roundabouts, the designers removed all other elements – buildings, footpaths etc – from the shots. The result is a quirky font with varied line widths and radii.

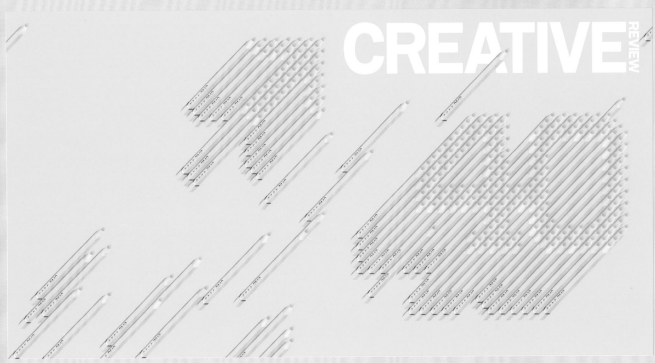

Design	RBG6
Project	Kada
Category	Font design / poster
Date	2002

The logo of a Raygil coffee machine provided the starting point for this caps-only stencil font. The original logo was probably based on a variant of Frankfurter. Kada was drawn from scratch without further reference to the Frankfurter font. A promotional poster was also produced, referencing the origins of the font by including a photograph of a polystyrene coffee cup spilling a thick black liquid which forms the letter 'A'.

Image
104

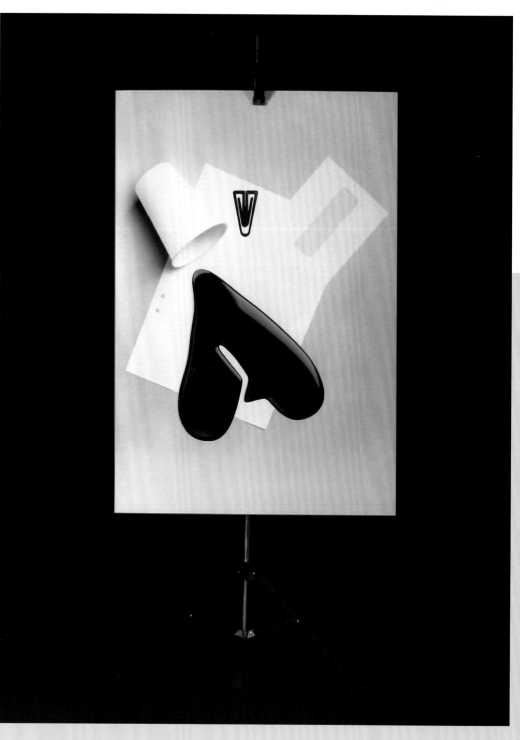

Design	Mode
Project	Happy New Year
Category	Greetings card
Date	2004

A simple folded sheet of high-gloss black paper is enlivened by the application of silver glitter to the custom-drawn typography. The geometric typography on this New Year's card from the London-based design consultancy is constructed from just a circle and a straight line. The design combines a retro Seventies disco aesthetic with a clean modern sensibility.

Design	RBG6
Project	Things to Do (2004)
Category	Installation
Date	2004

Based on one of the designer's own typeface designs, these New Year's resolutions have been sprayed onto the studio wall to serve as a semi-permanent reminder for the rest of the year.

Design	3 Deep Design
Project	Poster Magazine: Issue 10
Category	Magazine design
Date	2006

The font developed for issue 10 of the Australian fashion quarterly *Poster Magazine* is constructed from a complex grid of vertical, horizontal and 45-degree lines combined with semi-circles.

Design	3 Deep Design
Project	Poster Magazine: Issue 11
Category	Magazine design
Date	2006

This issue of the fashion quarterly uses highly elaborate letterforms created from old engraving plates that have been comped togther. The font is enhanced by very elaborate, digitally generated decorative borders.

MOONLIGHT SONATA

MINUTIAE

Design	Aufuldish & Warinner
Project	California College of the Arts
Category	Posters
Date	2004

Two very different posters for the same institution. On 'Art That Makes a Difference' (right) the calligraphic swirls and flourishes are all heavily digitally manipulated, revealing fragments of blurred imagery. The headline font, a bold condensed 1930s commercial American sans serif, serves as a counterbalance to the flowery background. A grittier urban approach is adopted for the second poster (below). Pages torn from an atlas form a background onto which 'Community Arts' and 'CCA' have been sprayed using a stencil font and then overlaid with lines of type set on yellow stripes.

Image
108

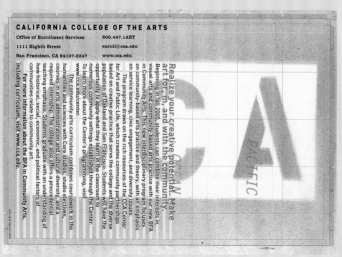

Design	Stiletto
Project	Alef Magazine
Category	Magazine design
Date	2006

A new high-fashion/lifestyle magazine concept for the Middle East, this English-language publication uses highly decorative arabesque illustrations and headline fonts offset by clean, modern, light sans-serif typography.

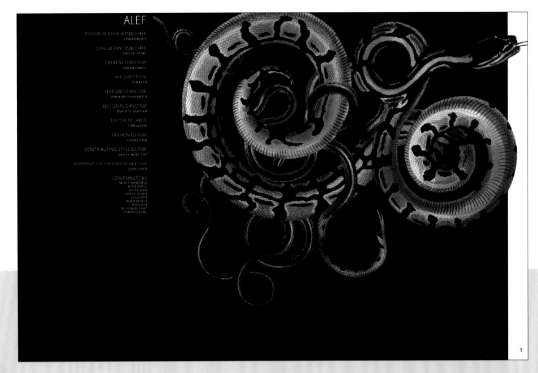

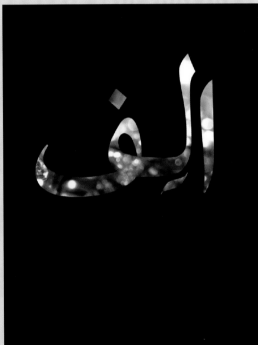

JUST AS ALEF TRANSLATES INTO THE LETTER A IN ARABIC, ALEF REPRESENTS THE FIRST MAGAZINE OF ITS KIND IN THE MIDDLE EAST. A FASHION, LIFESTYLE AND LUXURY TITLE, IT AIMS TO INFORM, INSPIRE AND ENTERTAIN READERS THROUGH A COMMITMENT TO THE HIGHEST LEVELS OF CONTENT AND DESIGN.

ALEF'S EDITORIAL MISSION IS THREEFOLD: TO BRING TOGETHER EMERGING AND ESTABLISHED ARTISTS IN AN EXPLORATION OF FASHION, LUXURY AND LIFESTYLE; TO SHOWCASE THE CULTURAL CONTRIBUTIONS OF THE REGION; AND TO CREATE AN AESTHETIC THAT CHALLENGES BOTH WESTERN AND MIDDLE EASTERN PRESUMPTIONS. ALTHOUGH DEVELOPED WITH THE SUPPORT OF VILLA MODA, ONE OF THE MIDDLE EAST'S MOST EMINENT RETAIL EMPORIUMS, ALEF IS NOT A "MAGALOGUE"—IT IS A COMPLETELY INDEPENDENT TITLE THAT WILL FEATURE EDITORIAL COVERAGE AND ADVERTISING FROM THE WORLD'S MOST PRESTIGIOUS LUXURY BRANDS. IT WILL LAUNCH ON A QUARTERLY SCHEDULE, WITH INTERNATIONAL DISTRIBUTION FOCUSING ON THE GULF REGION AND THE KEY FASHION MARKETS OF PARIS, LONDON, MILAN, TOKYO, NEW YORK AND LOS ANGELES AND OTHERS

ALEF REPRESENTS AN OPPORTUNITY TO POSITIVELY INFLUENCE CULTURAL UNDERSTANDING BETWEEN THE MIDDLE EAST AND THE WEST THROUGH AN EXPLORATION OF THE UNIVERSAL LANGUAGE OF BEAUTY. THE POWER OF THE MEDIA HAS A DEFINING IMPACT ON GLOBAL SOCIETY, AND IT IS OUR HOPE THAT, THROUGH THE APPLICATION OF HEARTFELT CREATIVITY AND INTELLIGENCE, WE CAN CONTRIBUTE TO THIS ONGOING DIALOGUE IN A GENUINE WAY.

IN ADDITION TO ITS AESTHETIC VALUE, THERE IS A COMPELLING FINANCIAL INCENTIVE TO PARTICIPATE IN ALEF. RECENT YEARS HAVE BROUGHT ABOUT A PARADIGM SHIFT FOR LUXURY BRANDS WHO RECOGNIZE THE IMMENSE MARKET POTENTIAL OF THE MIDDLE EAST. THE REGION'S CONSUMERS ARE RIVALED ONLY BY THE JAPANESE IN THEIR DESIRE FOR THE LATEST AND MOST EXTRAVAGANT LUXURY GOODS. BEAUTY AND STYLE HAVE A RICH AND STORIED

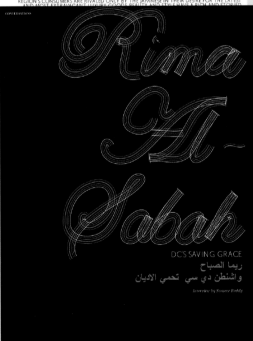

CONVERSATIONS

NOT MANY WOMEN CAN CLAIM U.S. SUPREME COURT JUSTICES, SENATORS AND CABINET MEMBERS AS REGULAR DINNER GUESTS, BUT FOR RIMA AL-SABAH, ONE OF WASHINGTON D.C.'S HIGHEST-PROFILE HOSTESSES, IT IS ALL PART OF THE JOB. MARRIED TO SHEIKH SALEM ABDULLAH AL-JABER AL-SABAH, THE KUWAITI AMBASSADOR TO THE UNITED STATES, SHE IS ONE OF THE FEW PEOPLE LEFT IN THE CITY WHO KNOW HOW TO THROW A FABULOUS PARTY WHILE SIMULTANEOUSLY SERVING A GOOD CAUSE.

D.C.'S SAVING GRACE

ريما الصباح
واشنطن دي سي تحمي الأديان

Interview by Sammar Boddily

Design	Non-Format
Project	The Wire
Category	Magazine design
Date	2001–2005

For four years Non-Format art-directed this long-established music monthly. A clean simple grid system and sans-serif body-copy style sheets were first established. The designers then created new headline fonts for nearly every number, while other issues used an existing font and welded distressed elements onto it. Over the four-year period the magazine retained an identity all its own through its creative use of experimental headline fonts, white space and excellent photography.

Image
110

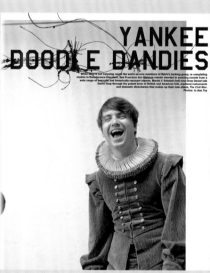

Although he's been a globally renowned artist for two decades, Mike Kelley's parallel career in music and sound art is a story rarely told. It is a tale that begins in Detroit with the post-Stooges punk noise insurgency of Destroy All Monsters, and winds up in Los Angeles via conceptual rock mythmaking with Tony Oursler in The Poetics, and collaborations with Sonic Youth, Scanner and Jean Beaublilard.
Words: Edwin Pouncey. Photos: Robert Gallagher

ANTI--ROCK CONSORTIUM

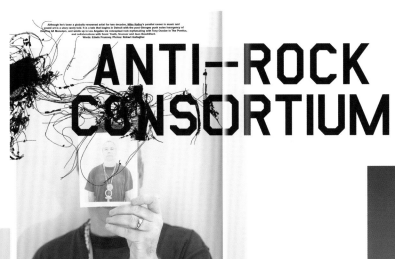

TUNNEL VISION

The Angels Of Light, formed in 1998 by Michael Gira as he emerged from Swans' long dark tunnel, might not be ebullitrashing like a train coming the other way, but their songs are no less intense just because he's 'gone acoustic'. In this New York interview, Gira explains how his more melodic new material is still shaped by his formative experiences in punk, transgression performance art and Glenn Branca's guitar orchestra, and explains how his Young God label has expanded to release artists such as Windsor For The Derby, Calla and outsider singer/songwriter Devendra Banhart.
Words: Alan Licht. Photos: Jo Ann Toy

THE WIRE 61

Founded nine years ago in response to bad European attempts to mimic Anglo American rock, Austria's Mego label have helped define the growth of experimental electronica in the 90s and beyond. In Vienna, Edwin Pouncey meets the label's inner circle, Ramon Bauer, Tina Frank and Peter Rehberg, to hear about the label's past, present and future. Photos: Magdalena Blaszczuk

THRIVING BY ACCIDENT

PETER REHBERG (TOP) AND HECKER IN VIENNA, MARCH 2×06

48 THE WIRE

THE BODY POLITI-CIAN

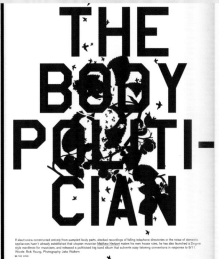

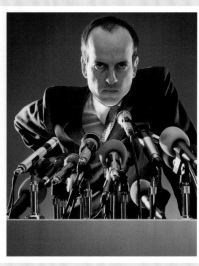

If electronica constructed entirely from sampled body parts, stacked recordings of falling telephone directories or the noise of domestic appliances hasn't already established that utopian musician Matthew Herbert makes his own house rules, he has also launched a Dogma style manifesto for musicians, and released a politicised big band album that subverts easy listening conventions in response to 9/11.
Words: Rob Young. Photography: Jake Walters

54 THE WIRE

Design   Non-Format
Project   The Wire
Category   Magazine design
Date   2001–2005

THE MASK OF SORROW

MF DOOM, KING GEEDORAH, VIKTOR VAUGHN, DANIELSAN, ZEV LOVE X... BEHIND THE METAL FACED MASK THAT BEARS A FIENDLY GRIN IS THE REAL DANIEL DUMILE? DUA KAN SHADOWS. ONE OF UNDERGROUND HIPHOP'S MOST MYSTERIOUS FIGURES IN ORDER TO PERPETRATE HIS CAST OF 'INVENTED' PERSONAE TO FIND THE ABDULAH HIPHOP EVER FDCD

TOMORROW NEVER KNOWS

AFTER MAKING TWO OF THE FINEST BUT OVERLOOKED APOCALYPTIC SINGER-SONGWRITER ALBUMS OF THE EARLY 70S – WITH JAZZ ARRANGER MIKE GIBBS AND FREE GUITARIST RAY RUSSELL – BILL FAY DROPPED OFF THE MAP, LEAVING LISTENERS TO SPECULATE WILDLY ABOUT HIS FATE. AS FAY'S CATALOGUE IS REISSUED THIS MONTH, ALONG WITH A PREVIOUSLY UNHEARD THIRD LP FEATURING GUITARIST GARY SMITH, ROB YOUNG DISCOVERS THE SINGER ALIVE AND WELL, AND STILL POURING OUT A RIVER OF SONG

THE WIRE 87

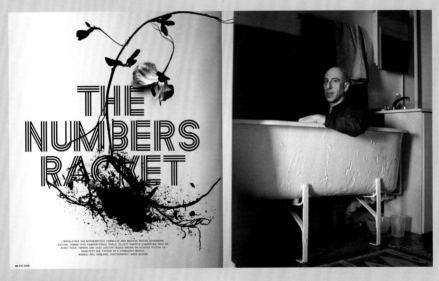

THE NUMBERS RACKET

TRANSLATING THE MATHEMATICAL FORMULAE AND MAGICAL RATIOS GOVERNING NATURAL FORMS INTO COMPOSITIONAL TOOLS, ELLIOTT SHARP'S CYBERPUNK TAKE ON AVANT ROCK, IMPROV AND 21ST CENTURY BLUES DRAWS ON SCIENCE FICTION TO ROAD-TEST HIS VISIONS OF A TURBULENT WORLD.
WORDS: PHIL ENGLAND. PHOTOGRAPHY: ANNA SCHORI

36 THE WIRE

PHANTOM POWER

THE LIGHTNING BALL OF ENERGY THAT IS MIKE PATTON SHOWS NO SIGNS OF LETTING UP. AS HE RANGES OVER AN EVER WIDER ARRAY OF HARDLINE MUSIC AND GROUPS INCLUDING FANTÔMAS, TOMAHAWK, MR BUNGLE AND HIS NEW COLLABORATIVE VENTURE PEEPING TOM, IN A SEARCHING INTERVIEW, THE VOCALIST REVEALS THE SOURCE OF HIS RELENTLESS DRIVE, HIS THOUGHTS ON HIS FRIEND AND MENTOR JOHN ZORN, AND THE RATIONALE BEHIND HIS ECLECTIC IPECAC LABEL.
WORDS: PHIL FREEMAN. PHOTOS: ROBERT GALLAGHER

Design	Non-Format
Project	Mara Carlyle
Category	Record sleeve / book
Date	2005

A variety of silhouetted flora and fauna are combined with the bold serif typography on designs for the musician Mara Carlyle. These motifs are further developed on the small book which accompanies the CD album, printed on very thin translucent onionskin paper of the kind used on old photograph albums to protect the images.

Design	Sagmeister Inc.
Project	Made You Look
Category	Poster
Date	2004

This poster was produced to promote an exhibition of work by the design company at the School of Visual Arts in New York and a newly published monograph. The stark, subtly manipulated portrait of the designers is set against a black flowery script, from which thin lines of ink run down the poster as if the type were bleeding. This 'bleeding' type also alludes to a famous poster by Sagmeister which features all the typography cut into the designer's bare chest with a razor blade.

Design	Non-Format
Project	Milky Globe
Category	Record sleeve
Date	2005

The initially neatly parallel and concentric lines of this Seventies-inspired font meander off into flowery motifs and journey over onto the back cover. Although in this way the lines become complex, the cover as a whole remains clean and focused. The elegant lines also migrate onto the label. The illustrated lines are drawn by Deanne Cheuk.

Design	Sagmeister Inc.
Project	Douglas Gordon: The Vanity of Allegory
Category	Book
Date	2006

The cover of this artist's book makes the most of the symmetry of the word 'VANITY' when written vertically. A 'V'-shaped wedge is cut into the book's boxed cover, with half of each letter printed on the left side running from top to bottom. The right side of this wedge is covered with a mirrored surface, so that when it is viewed at the correct angle the word becomes clear. The typography features elaborate swirls and flourishes similar to an illuminated manuscript. However, the calligraphic lines are given a digital feel by the fact that their thickness remains constant.

Design	Non-Format
Project	Hanne Hukkelberg
Category	Record sleeves
Date	2005

A bold condensed sans serif provided the starting point for the sleeves for these two releases by Hanne Hukkelberg. The type was then redrawn and elaborated by Si Scott. The results could easily have been a chaotic psychedelic mess, but use of a restricted palette of black and gold on a clean white background ensures instead that they have a very contemporary feel.

Design	Sagmeister Inc.
Project	School of Visual Arts
Category	Poster
Date	2005

The lettering on this recruitment poster for the School of Visual Arts in New York is formed from bent and manipulated twigs and branches set against an illustrated background that looks like it has come from the pages of a children's book.

Design	Sagmeister Inc.
Project	Everybody Thinks They Are Right
Category	Poster
Date	2006

This poster is another play on fantasy and reality. The designers were photographed at night in the act of relieving themselves. The elegant typographic statement was allegedly created from the two streams of urine.

Image
118

Design	Sagmeister Inc.
Project	Art Grandeur Nature
Category	Posters
Date	2004

The typography for this sequence of five posters reading 'Trying to Look Good Limits My Life' was created from found materials beautifully photographed in the landscape. As a result, the typography has both a natural and a man-made artificial quality.

type as experiment

The constant search for new forms results in designers
experimenting with the limits of typographic recognition
and legibility. Individual letters may initially appear as purely
abstract forms. However, when they are assembled together
with other characters, familiar shapes begin to emerge.

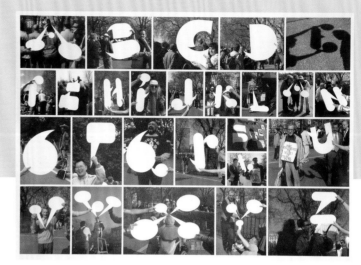

The pursuit of chaos

When looking for a challenging text, the reader's eye will be attracted to typography that avoids the discernible patterns which are the conventions of engagement between author and reader. An absence of these conventions – the formal rules of engagement – alerts, perhaps stimulates, the reader. Here is something different!

Unconventionally arranged experimental typography slows down the reader because it requires conscious participation. Compare this to conventional reading, a process so predictable that the reader is unaware of what is happening. Or how or why. Experimental type cannot be conventional and, therefore, will always demand more of the reader. An element of surprise or even shock is to be expected. Perhaps it is hoped for.

I think 'culture shock' is the appropriate description for a reader's emotional reaction when he or she is unable immediately to understand or predict an author's, or a typographer's, intentions. Such a state of mind is surely the intended outcome of experimental typography. The term 'culture shock', of course, is more commonly used to describe the sense of apprehension in a visitor to another country caused by unfamiliar environments and new social procedures or responses. This is recognized as a natural, physiological reaction, part of the routine process of adaptation to the shock of the unfamiliar and, to varying degrees, possibly the manifestation of a longing for a more predictable, more understandable and certainly less demanding, less experimental environment.

Here is a quote from an anthropologist in which he defines culture shock. As you read this short extract, consider the function of typography in magazines, on websites, on our streets and on our buildings:

'Culture shock is precipitated by the anxiety that results from losing all our familiar signs and symbols of social intercourse. These signs or cues include the thousand and one ways in which we orient ourselves to the situation of daily life: when to shake hands and what to say when we meet people… when to take statements seriously and when not… All of us depend for our peace of mind and our efficiency on hundreds of these cues, most of which we are not consciously aware'.[1]

When visitors' normal responses no longer appear helpful or even relevant, they tend to describe the signs, signals and customs of the host country as confusing, if not chaotic. (While inhabitants of the host country describe the visitor as ignorant.) It is natural for a visitor to feel anxious until he or she has had time to understand the social rules of engagement and learnt to act in an appropriate way. A different country, and a different culture, requires from the visitor a response, active participation, a questioning attitude and a consideration of adaptation and change. It is something of this kind that makes Julie Kim's blank speech-bubble alphabet so diverting (above). There are no clues in the bubbles, and so the viewer inevitably searches for narrative connections in the actions and facial expressions.

However, central to the concept of experimental typography is the question of the unpredictable and how readers adapt to it and are affected by it. For some, experience of the unfamiliar is entirely positive; indeed, it is often sought because coming to terms with the unexpected provides the opportunity to consider and (perhaps) adopt new values, attitudes and knowledge. 'The more one is capable of experiencing new and different dimensions of human diversity, the more one learns about oneself.'[2]

When a sense of adventure, of seeking out unfamiliar territory is cultivated by the typographer, then what are being promoted are ideals that equate novelty with value. Naturally, and surely to be expected of experimental typography, this is a demanding composite. Here, when working outside conventional cultural boundaries, idiosyncratic and iconoclastic goals are superior to objective and commonplace, orthodox ones. The design process in experimental typography is one of discovery and the reader must consent to the challenge in equal partnership with the author and/or the typographer.

The word 'must' is key in that last sentence because, for the reader, there is, of course, no alternative, except to refuse to read the unfamiliar-looking text. But once a decision has been made by the author and/or typographer to present a text in a particular (that is, experimental) way, its appearance and arrangement become an inextricable part of what is being communicated. (See the John Cage

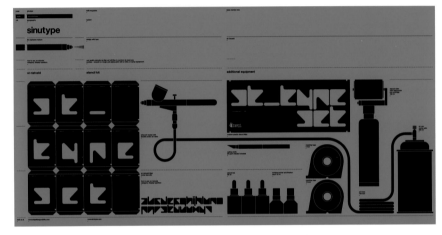

and Marshall McLuhan examples, far left and above.) Such a decision will, without doubt, reduce the size of a book's potential readership, but authors such as these have, from the outset, questioned the nature of communication and it is entirely appropriate that their texts, their means of communication, should test authority and be seen and acknowledged to be doing this at the same time as being read.

Naturally, for the reader, a text arranged in an unfamiliar way, or which uses an unfamiliar typeface, is impossible to take for granted. The reader's resulting agitated state of mind will, no doubt, be exactly what the author and/or typographer intended. When 'expression' becomes part of the textual communication process, all nominal notions of typographic 'good taste' become irrelevant. This is the area in which experimental typography flourishes. Here, it quickly follows that the conventional view of typography (that it should remain neutral, unaffected) cannot be, and would not wish to be, sustained.

Off the printed page the potential for heuristic letters constructing daft and sometimes deft messages is great. In urban environments, ephemeral typography is despised or celebrated – 'detritus or chance art'[3] – depending on the reader's point of view. 'Interference' by people making alternative, spontaneous additions or alterations (disregarding the best combined intentions of the architect, urban planner and typographer) is a necessary part of human interaction in any large community. Such ephemera may sometimes be considered ugly, but its purpose is generally to provide a valid source of information, even if only for a select few. Examples of entirely insignificant information, the 'detritus' of urban life, have proved to be a valuable source of evidence in recording social history. A city that grows organically and in accordance with the evolving needs of its inhabitants may appear to the visitor chaotic, but its human scale and eclectic mix also provide a unique and vibrant experience. The pity is that for the heroic-scale city architect, such a visceral experience can so easily be demolished on grounds of inefficiency, health and safety or, more likely, the authorities' inability to control it. This, of course, is what makes any form of 'non-standard' typography – be it conspicuously experimental or otherwise – interesting and relevant to its time. It must test the current lines of demarcation.

However, the printed ephemera of urban life is becoming less vernacular in character and is, rather worryingly, taking on a more familiar, more Helvetican appearance. In the past, major

experimental breakthroughs have often come from outside a discipline, because the 'experts' within tend to approach the discipline from a common, obedient point of view. The digital revolution will surely prove to be the most innovative period in the history of typography since the jobbing printer of the 19th century. But, for the seeker of vernacular, 'spur-of-the-moment' typography, the future looks less promising.

We are creative, we like to experiment, amuse, entertain and express ourselves. So, naturally, we leap at the opportunity to be self-indulgent when an open brief is offered - Stapelberg & Fritz's work for *Refill* magazine (above), for example, and many other pieces in this section. Trying to express ourselves in an original way is fraught with potential misunderstandings, but language (visual or linguistic) can also provide a group with a sense of partisanship. Academics from every field, street gangs and certainly typographers, all adapt language to the needs of their group. Since typography was democratized by digital technology, the language has widened, become less conservative, less precise. Meanwhile, the same technology has provided the typographer with the means to experiment. The rules of typography are described by every generation as being on the brink of disintegration and chaos. Somehow, so far, civilization has managed to remain intact, and the existence of experimental typography will continue to give proof of that fact.

1 K. Oberg, 'Culture Shock: Adjustment to New Cultural Environments', *Practical Anthropology*, 1960.

2 P.S. Adler, 'The Transitional Experience: An Alternative View of Culture Shock', *Journal of Human Psychology* 15, 1975.

3 Barbara Jones, writing about the photographs recording 'typographic detritus or chance art' on the streets of London by Herbert Spencer in 1963. *Typographica* n.s. 8.

Design	Andrew Byrom
Project	Interiors
Category	Sculptural typeface
Date	2002

This font crosses over from two- into three-dimensional forms. Each letter is physically created in welded square-profile tubular steel. The result is letterforms that are on the verge of becoming elements of furniture: 'b', 'd' and 'h' become chairs while 'm', 'n' and 'o' turn into tables.

Design	Daniel Eatock Associates
Project	Tapeface
Category	Packing tape
Date	2005

The designer created an uppercase-only font from standard brown packing tape, which was then scanned into a computer and converted into a digital typeface. This was subsequently printed onto clear packing tape, thus taking the process full circle. It can be taken one stage further still by creating new letterforms using Tapeface tape.

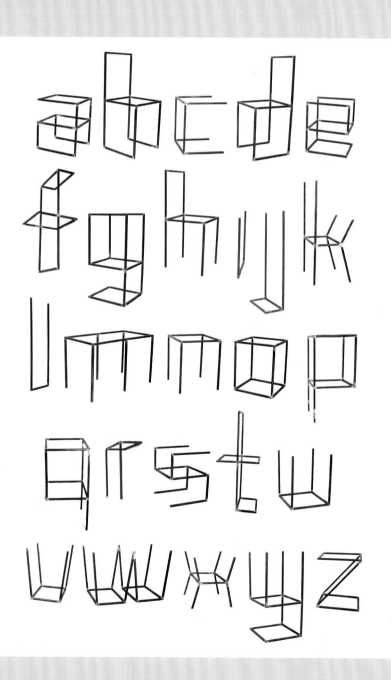

Design   Andrew Byrom
Project   Interiors Light
Category   Sculptural typeface
Date   2005

Based on the original Interiors font by the same designer (opposite), this variation puns on 'light' in typographic terms, transforming a reference to the line thickness of the characters into a series of neon-lit objects. The font makes a virtue of the tubular nature of neon signs as each character is formed from a single bent loop of glass tubing. As with the original Interiors font, some of the letters can work as freestanding objects while others require a little support.

Design	Andrew Byrom
Project	Concussion
Category	Font
Date	2000

A dot-matrix font which uses different-sized dots to form the characters. The font is based on the letter patterns used by eye doctors to determine colour blindness in a patient. Each letter not only uses different-sized dots but also draws on a palette of colours to give it greater depth.

Design	Andrew Byrom
Project	Bloodclot
Category	Font
Date	1997

Based on a selection of different-shaped plasters, the font creates an irregular pattern since there is no clear fixed baseline. The x-height also varies from character to character depending on the proportions of the original plaster used.

the everyday w●rld
is invisible
until we are forced to see it
differently ...
art is a primary means of making
strange the already seen,
already known

Victor Shklovsky, 1918

abcdefghijklmnopqrstuvwxyz
aBcdEFGHIJKLmnoPQRSTuvwXyz
1234567890

bloodclot

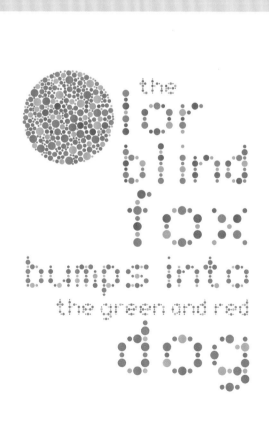

Design	RBG6
Project	No Time for Losers
Category	Poster / font design
Date	2004

Exhibition graphics and type design for 'No Time for Losers', a show by student curators at Stockholm University in Sweden, sent out as a folded A0 poster. The headline font was designed specifically for the poster, catalogue and exhibition graphics. Created from a series of rubberbands and pins, each letter was photographed and converted into line art. The final poster uses both line-art versions and the original black-and-white photographs.

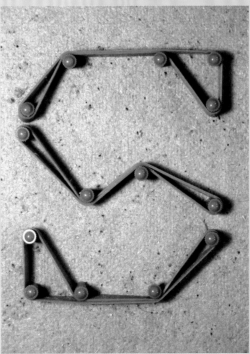

Design	Research Studios
Project	Made in Clerkenwell
Category	Identity / font / printed matter
Date	2003

Made in Clerkenwell is organized by the Clerkenwell Green Association, a body that supplies studio space to artists and creatives in the Clerkenwell area of London. This 'open studio' weekend is held to showcase the work of local artists and designers to the general public. Research Studios designed an identity for 2003's event based on a typeface specially created from a series of looped lines that fold and twist to form the letter shapes.

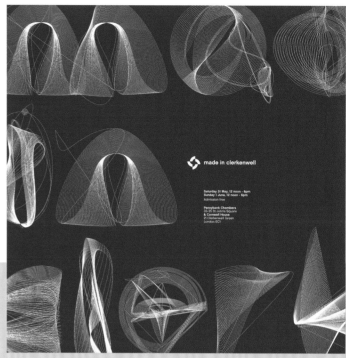

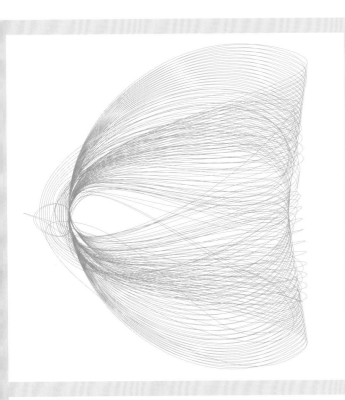

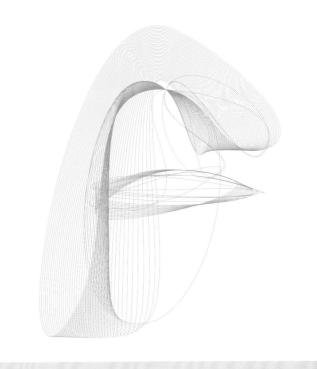

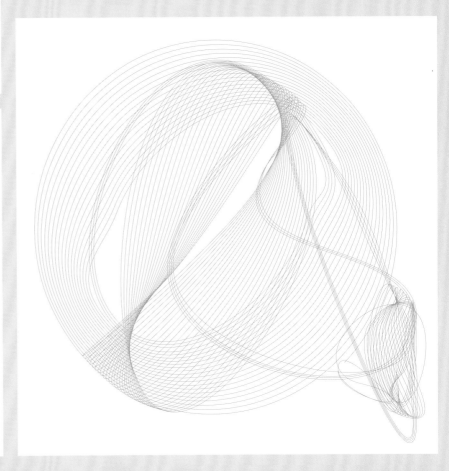

made in clerkenwell

Come to Clerkenwell Green Association's
studios and experience the best of craft &
design in action. Visit the studios, meet
designers, see demonstrations &
buy or commission unique pieces.

Saturday 31 May, 12 noon - 6pm
Sunday 1 June, 12 noon - 6pm
Admission free

Pennybank Chambers
33-35 St John's Square
& Cornwall House
21 Clerkenwell Green
London EC1

Nearest tube: Farringdon
(Circle, Hammersmith & City,
Metropolitan & Thameslink)

Bus routes: 55, 243

Tel: 020 7251 0276
Email: beatrice@cga.org.uk
Web: www.cga.org.uk

Clerkenwell Green Association is a unique charity
providing workspace, studios and business
support to craftspeople and designer-makers.
Charity no. 281415

Design	Alias
Project	RS&A Have Moved
Category	Mail shot
Date	2005

A moving card for Royse Sanders & Amfitheatreof, a company specializing in arts-related projects. Set in a bold condensed sans-serif font, the letters 'RS&A' morph into 'have', which then morphs again into 'moved'. As well as changing shape, the letters go through a spectrum of colours along their journey.

Design	Alias
Project	Creative Futures Exhibition
Category	Invitation
Date	2004

Created for an invite to an exhibition organized by *Creative Review* magazine, each character morphs into the next. The text reads: 'We are your future 15 stars of tomorrow in advertising and design.' The characters move around the page as well as morphing and changing colour, which gives the invite a dynamic energy.

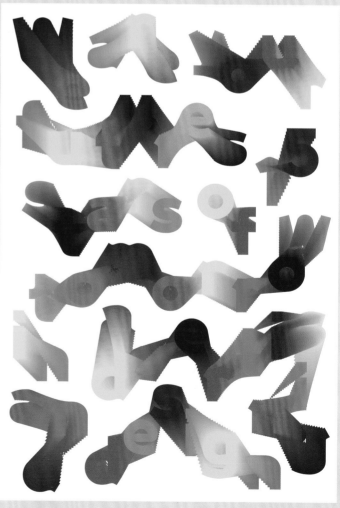

Design	CHK Design / Paul Beavis
Project	AF Metropolis
Category	Font / magazine cover
Date	2002

A digital typographic forest created for the cover of *Creative Review*. Each character of the masthead appears at the end of a long extruded base, evoking old hot-metal type where the letters are cast at the end of a long piece of lead. However, the stems of these letters become progressively wider towards the base, with characters twisting upwards like new shoots reaching up for sunlight.

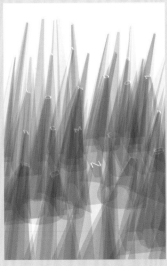

Design	Oded Ezer
Project	TypoArt
Category	Sculptures / posters
Date	2005

The designer uses both roman and Hebrew letterforms
to create complex biomorphic specimens. By modelling
creatures that are half-insect and half-letterform, he
explores the graphic extremes of legibility.

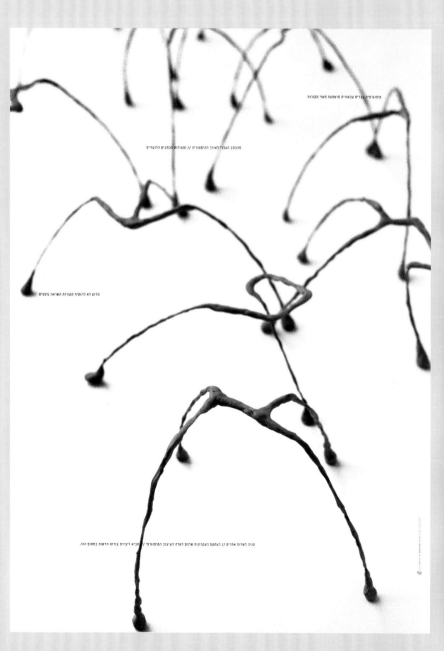

Design   Oded Ezer
Project   TypoArt
Category   Posters
Date   2005

As well as creating more conventional Hebrew typefaces,
the designer experiments with the ways in which
characters can be formed from folded paper and various
geometric shapes.

Design	Kapitza
Project	Blossomy
Category	Font
Date	2005

A pictographic font consisting of 72 flower and plant illustrations, these beautifully delicate silhouettes have no direct relationship to the letters on a keyboard. The PostScript font is simply a convenient way to access the vector-based illustrations, allowing the user to play with the illustrations in an easy manner.

Design	Kapitza
Project	East End
Category	Font
Date	2005

A pictographic font consisting of three sets, each containing 52 illustrations. As a contrast to the standard bold, roman and italic, they are called respectively Brick Lane, Liverpool Street and Victoria Park. These names refer to the locations in the East End of London where the original photography was carried out. From these photographs of people going about their daily routines, the designers then generated silhouettes and converted them into a digital font. The characters bear no obvious relationship to the letters on the keys that produce them.

Design	Hector Pottie
Project	One Two Thirty
Category	Font sampler
Date	2005

This brochure was produced to illustrate a new font. The designer chose to demonstrate the quirky characteristics of the face by simply writing out the numbers from 1 to 30. The brochure is screenprinted in white on a black board, folded but left unbound. The typeface has a strong retro Seventies feel, combining bold, rounded forms with hairline spaces.

Design	Hector Pottie
Project	Eins zwei fuenfundzwanzig
Category	Font sampler
Date	2005

This is based on the same principle as One Two Thirty (opposite), but this time the font is shown in an outline version. Again it is screenprinted, although on this occasion on pink card with magenta ink, the colours reflecting the more feminine, flowery nature of the font. The text counts from 1 to 25 in German. The outline version reveals some of the font's hidden intricacies, especially the internal circular elements.

Design	Julie Kim
Project	Bubblelogue
Category	Poster
Date	2005

Using classic cartoon speech bubbles as a starting point, the designer created a font that uses both positive and negative space. To promote her design, Kim took a set of large white speech bubbles to Speakers' Corner in London and asked members of the public to help re-create the characters for a photoshoot.

Design	Stapelberg & Fritz
Project	Dublex Inc: Eight Ears
Category	Record sleeve
Date	2004

Created from round-cornered rectangular blocks, this font manages to combine dense, solid forms with a light flourish. Complemented by a clean sans-serif font which is used for the bulk of information on this cover, the quirky headline face is restricted just to the title, which allows the strong photography more room to breathe.

Experiment

138

Design	Stapelberg & Fritz
Project	Pulverising til Sunrising
Category	Poster / advertising
Date	2004

Two variations of a poster/advertisement for a record-company club night in Berlin. The custom headline font uses thick strokes set with hairline spacing to create a bold, dense font. All other information is set in a clean bold sans serif that contrasts with the more challenging (from a reader's point of view) headline face.

Design	Stapelberg & Fritz
Project	Face to Face 5
Category	Poster
Date	2005

This headline font, based on that used on the Dublex Inc: Eight Ears record sleeve (opposite), serves almost as a form of abstract illustration on this poster promoting a design conference in Stuttgart.

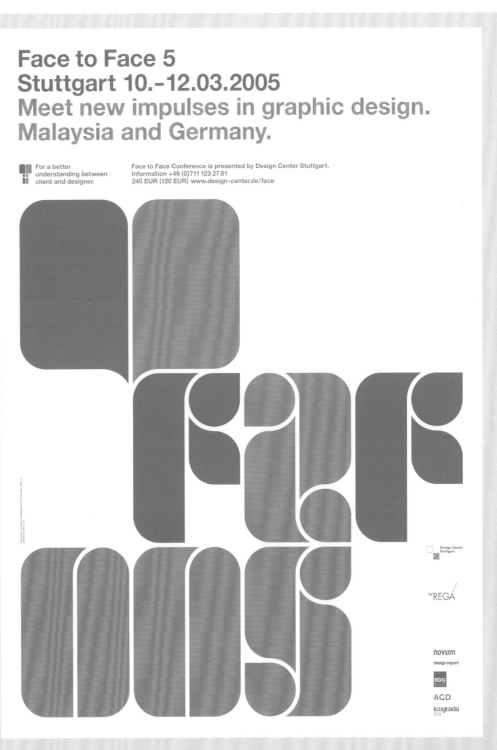

Design	Stapelberg & Fritz
Project	Refill
Category	Magazine spreads
Date	2005

The designers were commissioned by *Refill* magazine to produce a series of spreads. Since they were not given a specific brief or other editorial material to work with, they decided to develop a series of font experiments. The typefaces were designed for use as stencil fonts for different media, such as marker pens, airbrushes etc.

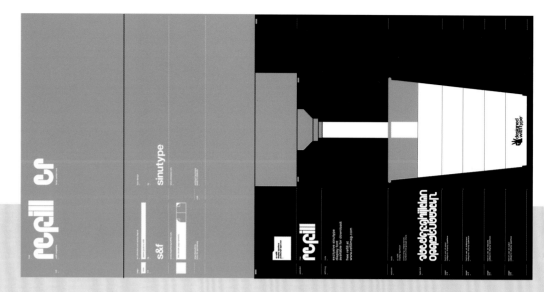

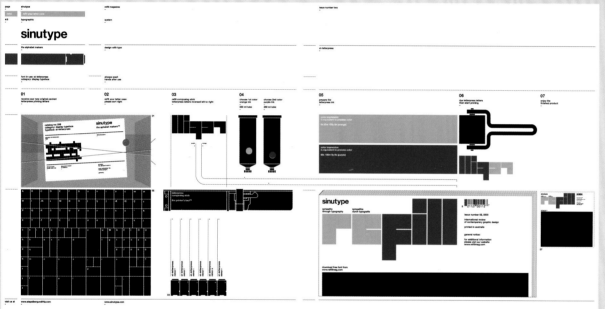

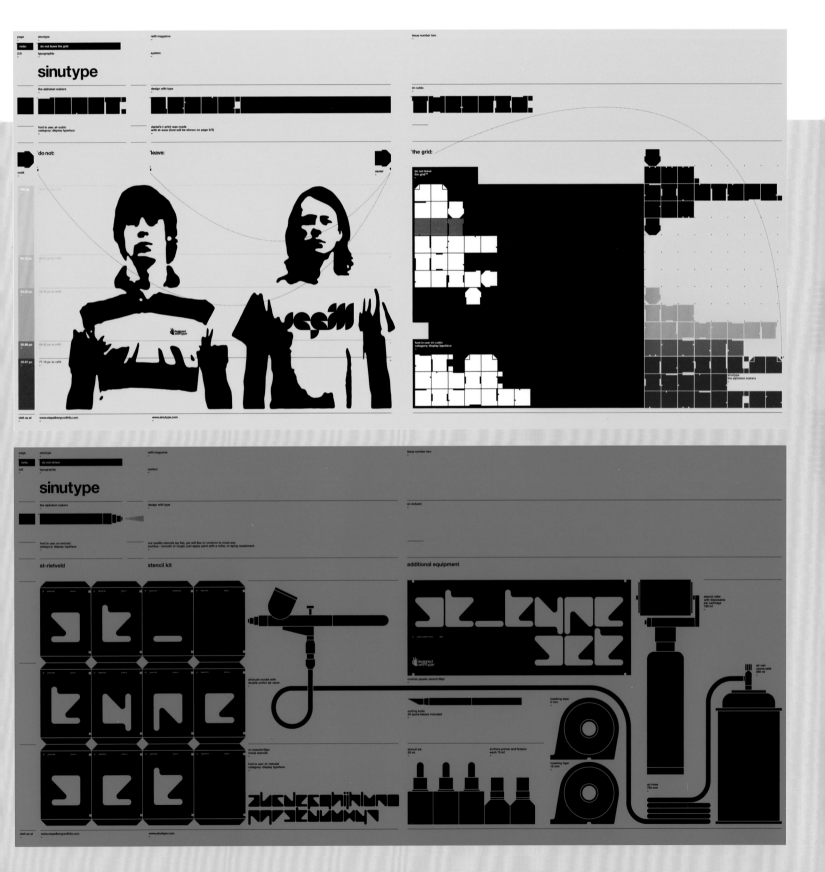

Design   SEA
Project   Wim Crouwel: Seen Unseen
Category   Catalogue
Date   2003

Produced to accompany an exhibition of Wim Crouwel's
posters from the late 1950s to the early 1970s, this
catalogue uses a font originally designed by Crouwel for
a show of work by American Pop artist Claes Oldenburg
but that has been digitally redrawn by The Foundry.
The face echoes Oldenburg's 'soft sculptures', which
converted everyday objects into larger-than-life soft PVC
versions of themselves.

Design	SEA
Project	The Typographic Circle Talk
Category	Poster
Date	2005

Produced to promote a talk by the designers, this poster uses blown-up fragments of their typographic work. Lavishly screenprinted, it features interwoven logo designs in different colours. Information is kept to an absolute minimum – the design company's name, the event, the date and the sponsor – and foil-blocked in silver, set very tightly in an extra-bold rounded font. There is no mention of location or time.

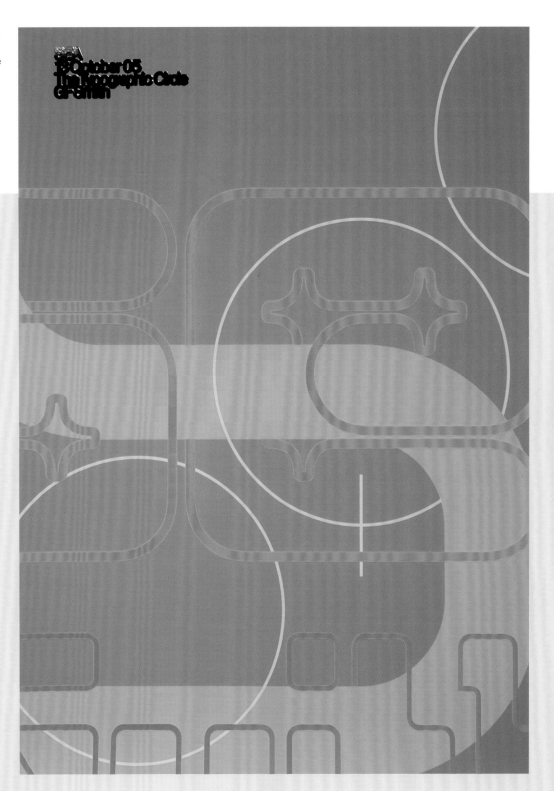

Design	Alias
Project	Mondo Grosso
Category	Record sleeve
Date	2005

A classic Bodoni typeface is combined with modern angular typographic forms in the cover design for this Japanese group. Although not instantly recognizable as alphabetic characters, the graphic shapes still preserve the essence of letter shapes. A series of diagonal lines extend out from the title, which form the foundations for the graphic shapes.

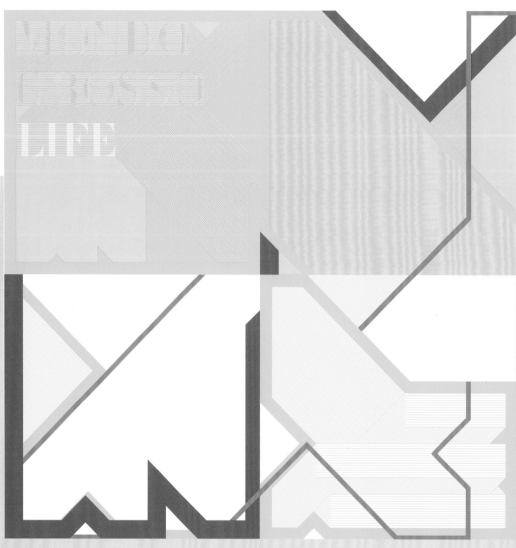

Design	Substance®
Typographers	Oscar Goldman, Neil Fletcher
Project	Somatic Responses
Category	Record sleeves
Date	2005

A series of record sleeves developed for an experimental electronic group, in which each uses pure typography to create rhythmic and arrhythmic patterns of distortion, while the simple black-and-white execution allows the pulsing typographic effects to come to the fore.

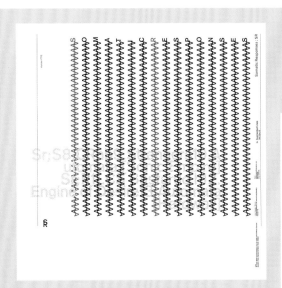

Design	3 Deep Design
Project	BalletLab – Fiction
Category	Poster
Date	2005

An isometric grid is printed over the lower three-quarters of this promotional poster for the BalletLab. The grid is created from a series of overlapping circles, their points of intersection forming its basis. Parallel lines set at 30 degrees are positioned at the intersections. This complex grid is used to generate the headline font for the poster. The hard-edged typography is softened by the introduction of a black-and-white image of a ballet dancer printed behind the white keylines of the grid.

Design	3 Deep Design
Project	Australian Paper – Impress
Category	Visual identity / printed matter
Date	2006

Impress is a luxurious range of gloss, matt and silk papers manufactured in Australia. The typography is formed from a highly complex grid system, a square unit divided up into 16 equal parts (4x4). These smaller squares are further divided with diagonals to create an octagonal form with a diamond shape inside. The units are then joined together to form the gridded font. This grid system is utilized in the company's printed collateral, with the grid becoming a key feature in press ads and printed promotional brochures.

ABCDEFHIJKLMNO
PQRSTUVWXYZ
abcdefghyklmno
pqrstuvwxyz
1234567890
.,;:!?OOI/-

impress.font.

Wanta
font to
impress?

log on and
download

——— To celebrate the redesign
of Impress, Australian Paper has released
a free limited edition Impress typeface.
——— Simply log onto
www.australianpaper.com.au for more
information and download details.

——— Designed by 3 Deep Design
and constructed by Dalton Maag Ltd (UK)
the intricate and detailed Impress
typeface signals a new way of thinking
for Impress and a commitment to great
Australian Design.

——— The Impress range is the
only A2 coated paper manufactured right
here in Australia and delivers a comprehensive range of grammages in Silk, Matt
and Gloss finishes.
——— To download the Impress
Font log on to www.australianpaper.com.au
For information and samples of Impress
contact Dalton Fine Paper or Spicers
Paper today.

Australian Paper

impress.

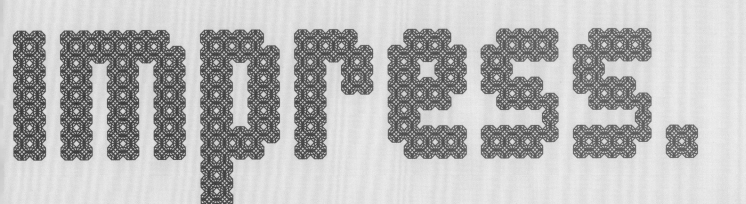

Design	3 Deep Design
Project	BKK Architects
Category	Visual identity / stationery range
Date	2005

The identity for this Australian architectural practice is formed from a complex grid system derived from a series of interlocking circles. A diamond shape is formed at the intersections, which is the basic shape for the dot-matrix font. The identity has been produced in three different weights: varying the proportions of the diamond-shaped dot causes the letterforms to become heavier or lighter. The letterhead prints a dot-matrix grid full-bleed on the reverse side, with a mirror image of the identity printed white out. The restrained typography on the front of the letterhead is enhanced by the subtle show-through of the logo from the back.

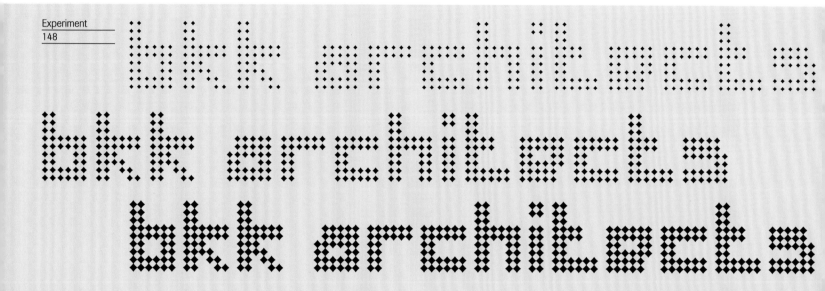

Design	Cartlidge Levene
Project	Architects Registration Board
Category	Visual identity / annual report
Date	1999

Design	BB/Saunders
Project	Jason Bruges Studio
Category	Visual identity / stationery
Date	2005

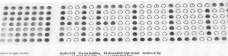

The new logo for the Architects Registration Board (ARB) is formed from a custom-made dot-matrix font. The centres of the dots are set close together, which means the circles overlap and create a very tight, concentrated version of a dot-matrix font. The grid formed by the interlinking circles is used as a background in the annual report. Halftone images printed in a darker yellow appear inside these circles, giving the impression of a very coarse halftone screen.

A grid of 7x7 dots forms an abstract logo for this London studio which specializes in creating screen-based installations, interactive light sculptures and events. The stationery range features a matrix of small laser-cut holes which cast shadows as a simple illustration of light and shadow. As well as the 7x7 grid of holes, the letterhead also includes a section with semi-punched holes: the user is thus able to punch out dots to create dot-matrix words.

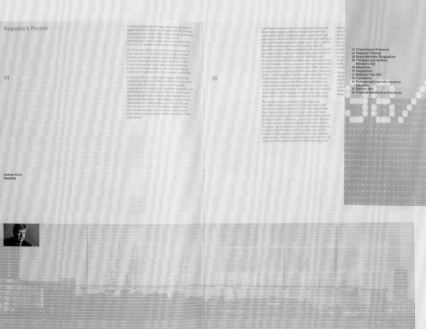

Design	Wig-01
Project	Previous / Next
Category	Book
Date	2006

This self-promotional book combines commercial commissions with self-initiated experiments, including many typographic ideas. The latter range from digitally generated sketches to more hands-on experiments, such as type formed from elastic bands and dot-matrix fonts created by punching holes in the paper's surface.

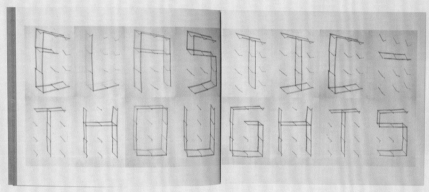

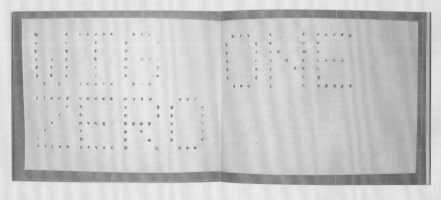

Design	CHK Design
Project	How Do You Look?
Category	Exhibition
Date	2004

The designer created all visual elements, from posters to exhibition graphics, for a show about visual cognition in painting and surgery at the Dulwich Picture Gallery in London. The specially developed dot-matrix font uses the dots at different brightness levels to create a sense of the characters drifting towards and away from the surface.

HOW DO YOU LOOK?

Visual cognition in painting and surgery
A Wellcome Trust 'Engaging Science' project directed by John Tchalenko

5 October – 21 November 2004

Dulwich Picture Gallery
Gallery Road • London SE21 7AD • 020 8693 5254
www.dulwichpicturegallery.org.uk

Tuesday – Friday 10am–5pm • Saturday & Sunday 11am–5pm

FREE ADMISSION • • •

Design	Kapitza
Project	What Does It Mean When a Whole Culture Dreams the Same Dream?
Category	Art catalogue / series of posters
Date	2004

For an exhibition of work by three text-based artists – Volker Eichelmann, Roland Rust and Johannes Schweiger – the designers produced a series of 15 large posters, each with the text printed in a single colour and using the same dot-matrix font for the entire project. The font is simply constructed from a square base element, which allows the typeface to be scaled up and down and to maintain a relationship with other letters at different sizes. The catalogue accompanying the exhibition was formed by cutting, folding and binding together the 15 posters, thereby making catalogue and exhibition one entity.

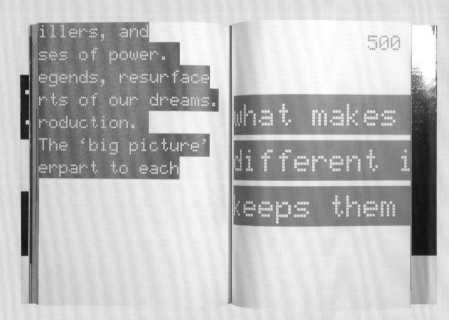

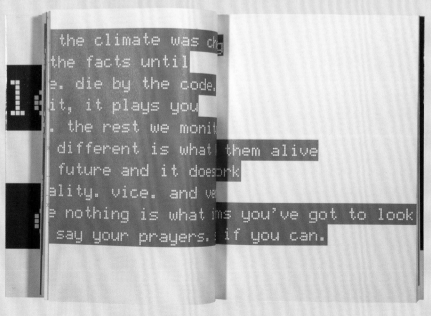

Design	Spin
Project	Dan Flavin: Works from the 1960s
Category	Postcard pack
Date	2005

This was produced to accompany an exhibition of the artist's fluorescent-tube light sculptures from the 1960s held at the Haunch of Venison gallery in London. The designers created a font that mirrored the artist's aesthetic. This typographic styling was used to promote the exhibition and also on a postcard pack, where the typography wraps round the outer slipcase of the pack.

Design	SEA
Project	The Architecture Foundation:
	Mars Pants
Category	Poster / catalogue
Date	2001

A grid of small white dots is printed out of the entire surface of the poster and the catalogue cover, with the background printed as a graduation tint running from 10% to 100% of a dark purple. As such, the white dots appear clearer towards the bottom of the poster. Key words related to the exhibition are created by removing white dots to form letters in a basic dot-matrix font. All other typography is tightly set in Univers.

Design	3 Deep Design
Project	Punch Out: Material By-Product
Category	Catalogue
Date	2006

Material By-Product is a new fashion collaboration formed by Susan Dimasi and Chantal McDonald. This beautiful brochure features a foil-blocked oversized cover. The elaborate typography is generated from the sequence of overlapping circles which create a grid system. The typeface has an irregular form and a highly stylized decorative quality. Fragments of the title appear on the front cover: these are in fact the counters from the letterforms (the internal spaces of the 'P', 'O', 'A', 'R' and 'D'). On the inside front cover the full title appears, but here the counters are filled in.

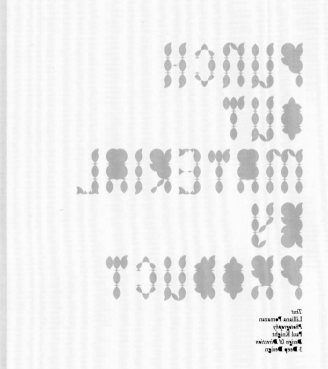

Text
Lilliana Pomazan
Photography
Paul Knight
Design & Direction
3 Deep Design

Design	A2/SW/HK
Project	Eyes, Lies + Illusions
Category	Exhibition graphics
Date	2004

This was created for an exhibition at the Hayward Gallery in London about the use of optical tricks and illusions in art. The designers produced two new fonts, an optically challenging headline one and a more conventional one for additional text. The characters in the headline font have a simple bitmap form which is enhanced by the use of diagonal black-and-white stripes which run over the entire surface. The lines change direction whenever they hit the edge of a character. The effect is pure Op Art. The text font has the characteristics of an OCR (Optical Character Recognition)-style font.

Design	Studio Philippe Apeloig
Project	Typo / Typé
Category	Poster
Date	2005

These two posters were designed to publicize exhibitions of work by the French type designer, one held at the Carré Sainte Anne, Montpellier, and the other at the Museum of Russian Art in Kiev, Ukraine. Both posters are generated using the same typographic construction methods: the letters are formed by a series of diagonal lines or slashes in different thicknesses.

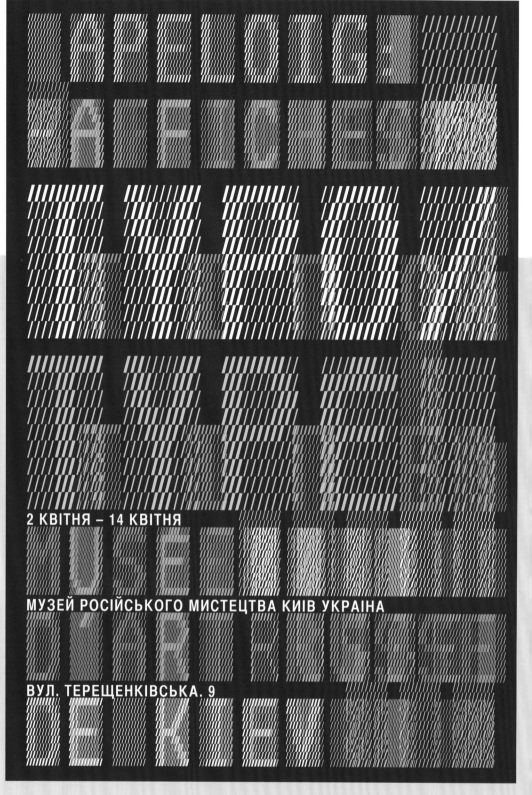

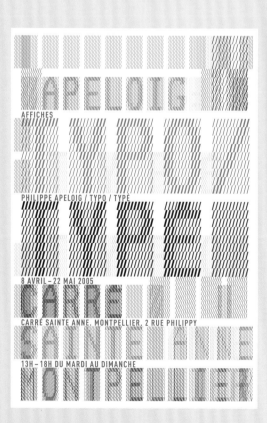

Design	CHK Design
Project	AP Book Series
Category	Visual identity / printed matter
Date	2005

The AP logo is generated from a matrix system which reflects the more practical and engineered aspect of architecture that the series illustrates. The matrix font is also used inside for headlines and chapter openers.

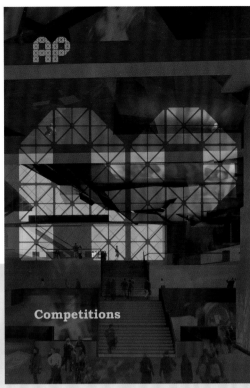

Publicity

Competitions

CONTENTS

Axel Schultes/Charlotte Frank
(Berlin, Germany)
German Chancellery Building
Berlin, Germany
Invited Competition 1994
Completion 2001

Interior perspective

Government Buildings

Design   Andrew Byrom
Project   Byro Stencil
Category   Typeface
Date   2000-2002

This font is designed in three variants: Block, Round and Square. Although they are visually quite different, all three were generated as stencil fonts, allowing them to be die-cut out of a material and sprayed, painted or drawn onto a surface. The designer has generously made the fonts available as free downloads from his website.

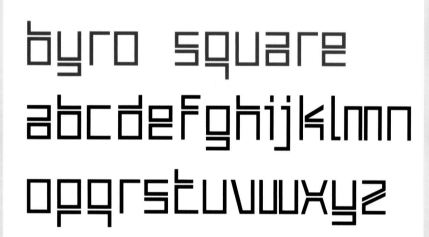

Design	Andrew Byrom
Project	Website announcement
Category	Typeface / mailer
Date	2005

A very simple cutter is used to generate a font for this mailer. Using only straight lines, the characters are created with all internal spaces forming rectangular holes.

Design	Andrew Byrom
Project	St. Auden
Category	Typeface
Date	2005

Another stencil-based font, this time more delicate and subtle in form. The font was created for the designer's son in order to help him gain a good understanding of typography from a young age. It was also distributed as a clear plastic stencil sheet, reminiscent of those found in every child's pencil case.

Design	Saturday
Project	Blaak
Category	Visual identity / applications
Date	2005

This elegant identity for the fashion label Blaak cuts and slices up the bold sans font (Avant Garde) to create new abstracted elements from the letter shapes, which are both familiar and alien.

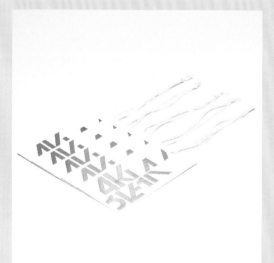

Design	Mode
Project	Dalton Maag: Font Book Collection 01
Category	Catalogue
Date	2004

This font catalogue focuses on four type families designed by the typefoundry Dalton Maag. Each font is shown in a variety of weights and combinations of size for text and headline setting. The text pages are printed on very light bible paper, which allows for a great deal of show-through. All the text pages have a series of vertical perforated lines running down them, positioned in accordance with the typographic grid. These perforations allow the user either to fold back pages to show different combinations of weights and sizes, or to tear out perforated strips for use as sample swatches.

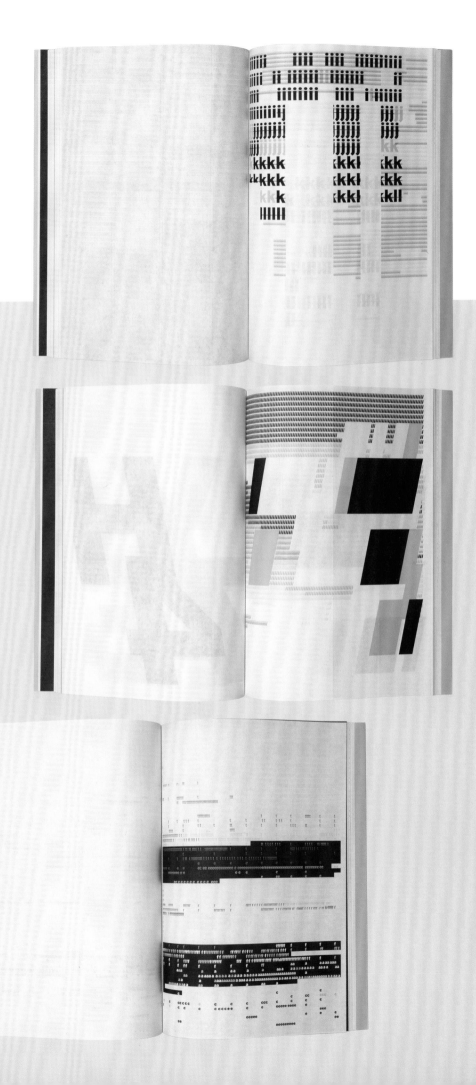

type in motion

When placing typography in a physical, three-dimensional environment, the designer needs to consider how the letterforms will appear from a variety of angles, so opening up a multitude of new typographic possibilities. A similar potential exists with screen-based type, which allows the designer to work both within time and a 'virtual' depth of field.

The pursuit of order

So much information is delivered on the move. Either the information is moving or the reader is moving. And sometimes both. Being able to do two things at the same time gives the impression of additional speed, efficiency and effectiveness. Motion itself attracts, something recognized by the owners of advertising hoardings and demonstrated by many of the examples shown on the following pages. Where the type does not physically move, at least the suggestion or effect of motion comes alluringly into play.

The urban environment is awash with type that is required to be read in motion. Improvised information, hastily positioned in city streets, is generally considered to be visual clutter. Its untidy (that is, uncoordinated) appearance is simply the consequence of expediency. Traffic diversion signs are, of course, particularly unpopular because they present a disruption and portend, at the very least, an unplanned and extended journey, perhaps requiring the negotiation of unfamiliar territory. However, if such signs are coordinated in appearance and placement, the level of anxiety will be reduced because the diversion will be perceived as an orderly response to a scheduled event. In other words, the driver will assume that this is a planned, rather than an ad hoc and hurried, emergency-induced event.

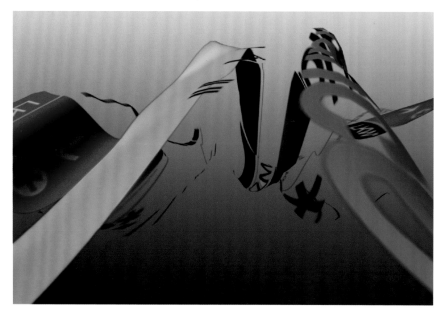

But when a genuine emergency occurs, it is reassuring to see a coordinated effort to re-establish order, usually in the form of hastily erected signs, with access inhibited by tape and barriers. Coordination of these elements is important because order suggests authority. And 'authority' knows it needs to be seen to be in control. Enforced change (for whatever reason) is stressful because an alteration to our daily routine forces us to think about activities that we would normally be able to take for granted. It makes us think about the mundane things that have to be done – emergency or not! Routine allows us to think about other, more selfish, more creative things.

Patterns provide predictability. Predictability in typographic presentation diminishes the fear of unfamiliar territory for the reader. It follows that formal design helps to overcome the problems of transmitting difficult (less predictable) information. Alternatively, it also allows a simple message to be communicated in a complex way (for instance, The Future of Croydon, above.) If the intended audience is larger and more heterogeneous, then a certain formality of presentation is essential. If, however, the audience is more specialized – and therefore, perhaps, attuned to a particular typographic delivery – then it might be reached with what could seem to others to be a more challenging (less predictable) mode of presentation, for example, allowing the rhetoric of systematic typography to be turned into amorphous, liquid fragments of typography (Lewis Kyle White's self-initiated project, left).

Conventional typography reduces the effort required to comprehend. Comprehension is the reason for all aspects of reading. We learn the various reading skills necessary for acquiring differing kinds of information. In addition to the basic mechanics of reading, we also learn to adjust our approach when taking in typographic information on the move. The ability to recognize the natural purpose of information, read it quickly and, as a result, be able to make an appropriate decision, depends very much on the organization and systematic arrangement of typography being standard.

Typically, in books, standard arrangements for specialist information are achieved by using the full family of typefaces in a text fount: bold, italic, small caps etc. The application of a grid also becomes more significant when the information becomes potentially more complex. The absolute order of a dictionary or encyclopedia, in which

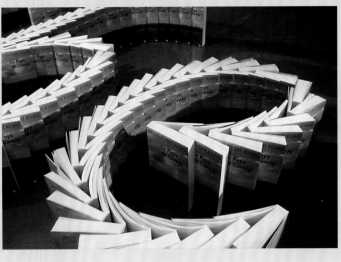

everything has its rightful and logical place, undoubtedly provides such documents with an implicit sense of power and substance. But all books, even the humble paperback, carry authority and so the notion of transforming them into a word (Typeworkshop.com, above right) rather than the usual transformation of words into a book, makes a poignant statement. The full word (on page 173) spells an elegant 'Liberté'.

Type on buildings attains its power by association with the material into which it is carved or to which it is otherwise attached as much as the letterforms themselves. Order and power are linked in so many ways, and the idea of a fixed place being a condition of authority is surely an intrinsic part of this. Place (and the 'right' to be there) is linked with status.[1] Logic dictates that if a *laissez-faire* statement of transience is appropriate, then temporary materials, such as wooden freight palettes, might be effective (page 171). All the signage for the Parc La Villette, designed by Intégral Ruedi Baur et Associés, 'plays' a similar temporal game (above).

This recognizable precision and predictability of structure is essential for democratic access to information. The status of the printer and the typographer was linked to place by Beatrice Warde in her famous broadsheet *This Is a Printing Office*, written and designed in 1932 to display Eric Gill's Perpetua Titling for the Monotype Corporation. Here are the first few lines to provide a flavour: 'This is a printing office, crossroads of civilisation, refuge of all the arts against the ravages of time, armoury of fearless truth against whispering rumour.'

Interestingly, Warde also links status with time. Natural phenomena (mountains, sunsets etc) are venerated for their seeming immortality, but man-made monuments, buildings, crossroads, tools, artifacts, in fact, anything that provides us with a link to previous human endeavour, also fill us with wonder. And clearly the status of these increases with their age. Something designed to resist 'the ravages of

time' must surely have been considered important? Today, designing something, anything, that is intended to last longer than its maker's lifetime is becoming a rare occurrence. As a result, our sense of order, our place and status in the world, is diminished. It's not surprising, then, that type in motion, generally, is designed with a specific lifespan and a limited purpose in mind.

First the telephone, then the radio and television, and now the internet have provided us with an entirely different sense of time and place. These mediums can all be accessed on the move. Certainly, politicians and other figures of authority can no longer speak exclusively from a position or place of power: the steps of the Roman Senate, the church pulpit or the lectern. In fact, with the mass implementation of CCTV, none of us any longer has control of our image. However, those who want and have the 'means' (money, influence) to control their image still go to great lengths to do so. Meanwhile, the public are becoming highly attuned to (and entertained by) the strategies adopted by an individual or an organization to control the media and the image it conveys of them.

'The desire to remove human error, clear human confusion and diminish human misery' was how Matthew Arnold described the function of art in 1869.[2] The nature, variety and influence of the mass media today have sent art in a very different direction, but Arnold's definition might still be appropriate to what the typographer has in mind when type has to be read while in motion.

The value of order and the possibility that it might provide our daily lives with greater clarity undoubtedly remain the reason why society has placed so much value on it. The status of lettering on buildings was certainly built upon it. Even today, when the materials and method of construction might be different and, generally, less permanent, type designed to be read in motion has never been more prominent.

The systems we use every day to organize the things we design, be they the modular units for an office building or a grid governing text layout, are based upon the assumption that order stabilizes and clarifies. But it can also stultify. To really appreciate the pursuit of order one also needs to consider the pursuit of chaos. 'Type in Motion' provides ample evidence of typographers harnessing the attributes of chaos to attract a readership.

1 Following the popularity of *This Is a Printing Office*, Beatrice Warde wrote and designed several other broadsheets conveying similar sentiments. These include: *Here We Have Built a School of Printing* and *Pause Stranger: You Stand in a Composing Room*. There were many variations written and printed that were based upon the original *This Is a Printing Office*. The *Monotype Recorder* 44:1, 1970, records most of these.

2 Matthew Arnold, *Culture and Anarchy*, 1869.

Design	FL@33
Project	AAT – Animated, Acoustic Typefaces
Category	Font
Date	1999–2001

A font collection that explores different typographic qualities and possibilities when used in print and on screen. The interactive application was finished in early January 2001 for the Royal College of Art 'Work in Progress' exhibition. There are three typefaces: Delayed, Unfolded and Binary. Each is available in different sound and animation modes. By using mouse and keyboard, you can play and write with the application. The AAT application can be downloaded for free at www.flat33.com.

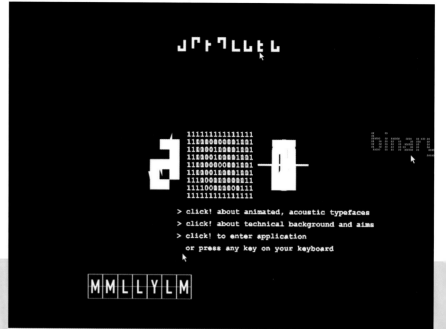

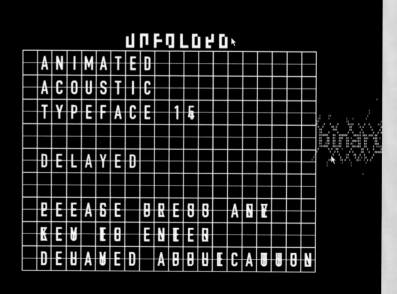

Design	FL@33
Project	Self-initiated
Category	Typeface
Date	2004

This font is based on a mechanical typeface found on signage and information displays all over Paris. The designers have produced animated sequences to show how it could be used in different environments.

Design	Studio for Virtual Typography
Project	The Future of Croydon
Category	Signage / public sculptures
Date	2004

This concept for a series of public sculptures was developed for Croydon Council in Surrey, England. The project set out to explore the possibilities for civic branding by means of the exclusive use of a specific font. The three-dimensional sculptural letterforms are constructed from a series of tubular metal elements that appear to transform themselves from abstract sculptural elements to full letterforms as the viewer moves past them.

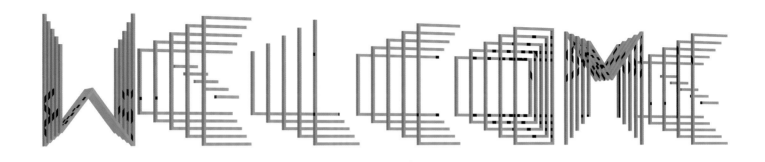

Design	Intégral Ruedi Baur et Associés
Project	Parc La Villette
Category	Visual identity / signage
Date	2005

The design of the visual identity for this French site extends to all aspects of signage, for both temporary and permanent events. Large three-dimensional letterforms are planted on poles which visitors walk past on their travels. Huge megagraphics are also employed on the façade of the building, while more transient information pods are constructed from recycled wooden freight palettes.

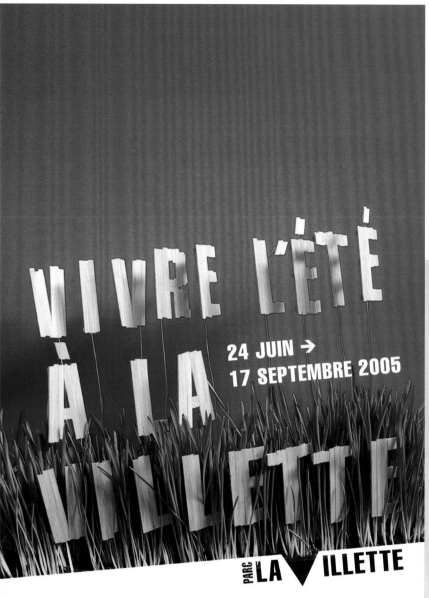

Design	Typeworkshop.com
Project	Movable Type / Manual Pixelism / Let It Run
Category	Installations
Date	2005

Typeworkshop.com originates from workshops given by
Underware, a graphic design studio based in Holland and
Finland that specializes in designing and producing
typefaces. The workshops help the participants to
understand typography more fully in a physical sense.
'Movable Type' used cardboard boxes as its construction
material. 'Manual Pixelism' created pixel-based fonts from
repeated modules, such as disposable plastic drinking
cups, supermarket shopping trolleys and paperback books.
'Let It Run', meanwhile, was constructed as the world's
biggest type-domino.

Design	Precursor
Project	MTV Networks International
Category	TV ident
Date	2005

Using the empty bowels of a cargo ferry as a background, this TV ident for MTV Networks International features digitally generated typography that constructs itself from abstract modules. Fragments fly into view and morph into three-dimensional letterforms.

Design	Lewis Kyle White
Project	Graduate School of Arts, Culture and Environment
Category	Poster
Date	2005

The different disciplines available at the Graduate School of Arts, Culture and Environment are constructed out of three-dimensional letterforms for this poster for the University of Edinburgh. An aerial shot of the city, printed in green and black, forms the background against which the thin white grid lines used for the construction of the headline typography are visible. A different colour is employed for each subject, which helps legibility since the letters otherwise become interwoven over the poster.

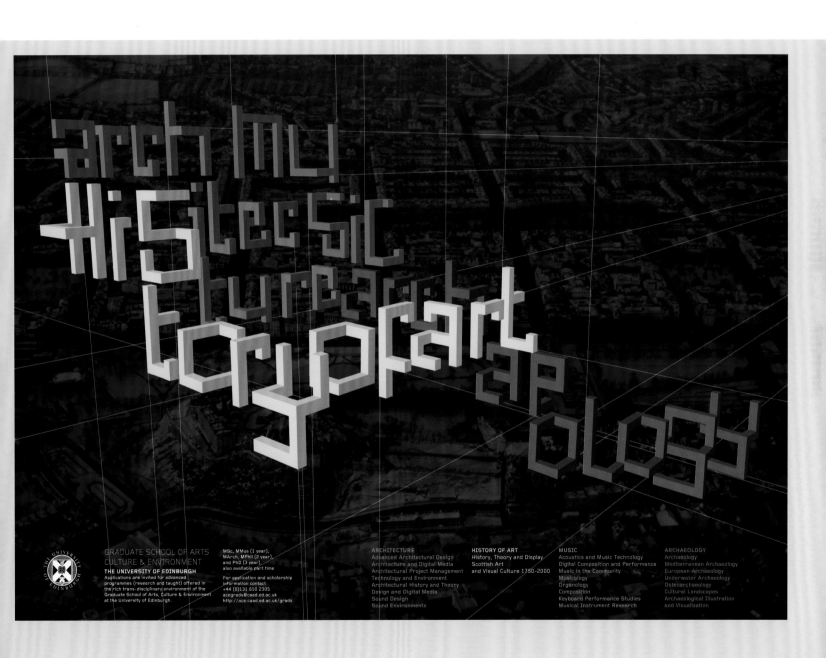

GRADUATE SCHOOL OF ARTS
CULTURE & ENVIRONMENT
THE UNIVERSITY OF EDINBURGH
Applications are invited for advanced
programmes (research and taught) offered in
the rich trans-disciplinary environment of the
Graduate School of Arts, Culture & Environment
at the University of Edinburgh.

MSc, MMus (1 year),
MArch, MPhil (2 year),
and PhD (3 year),
also available part time

For application and scholarship
information contact
+44 (0)131 650 2305
acegrads@caad.ed.ac.uk
http://ace.caad.ed.ac.uk/grads

ARCHITECTURE
Advanced Architectural Design
Architecture and Digital Media
Architectural Project Management
Technology and Environment
Architectural History and Theory
Design and Digital Media
Sound Design
Sound Environments

HISTORY OF ART
History, Theory and Display
Scottish Art
and Visual Culture 1750-2000

MUSIC
Acoustics and Music Technology
Digital Composition and Performance
Music in the Community
Musicology
Organology
Composition
Keyboard Performance Studies
Musical Instrument Research

ARCHAEOLOGY
Archaeology
Mediterranean Archaeology
European Archaeology
Underwater Archaeology
Osteoarchaeology
Cultural Landscapes
Archaeological Illustration
and Visualization

Design	Stiletto
Project	Balloon Animals
Category	Film title sequence
Date	2005

A sequence of thin balloon string-like lines drift across a
pale white cloudy sky and form joined-up writing for the title
sequence of this film by Michael Karbelnikoff. They ravel
and unravel themselves into the different bits of information
before the film's title finally appears and then drifts off again
as the camera pans down from the sky into a building to
signal the beginning of the film proper.

Mark Boone Jr

Seymour Cassel

Balloon

Balloon Animals

Design	Adam Hayes / Henry Hobson
Project	Norway
Category	Film
Date	2005

Hand-drawn typography 'grows' out of a backdrop of forest undergrowth. Some text elements appear to float around the darkened woods, while other bits of typography snake their way around the moss-covered forest floor.

Design   Stiletto
Project   VH1 Soul
Category   TV ident
Date   2005

Two ten-second idents for the music channel VH1 Soul.
The loose hand-drawn typography is flexible enough to
lend itself to significantly different treatments.

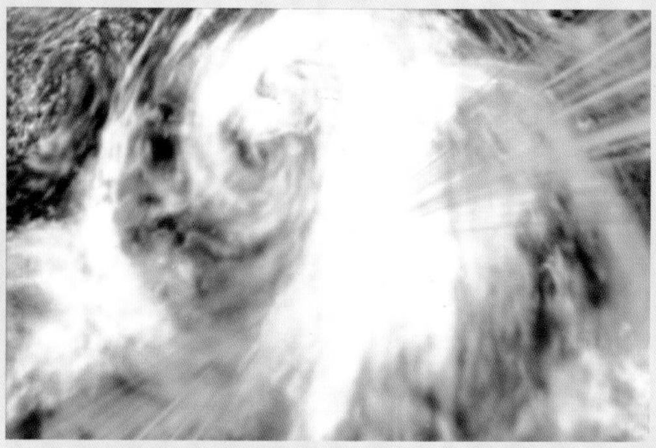

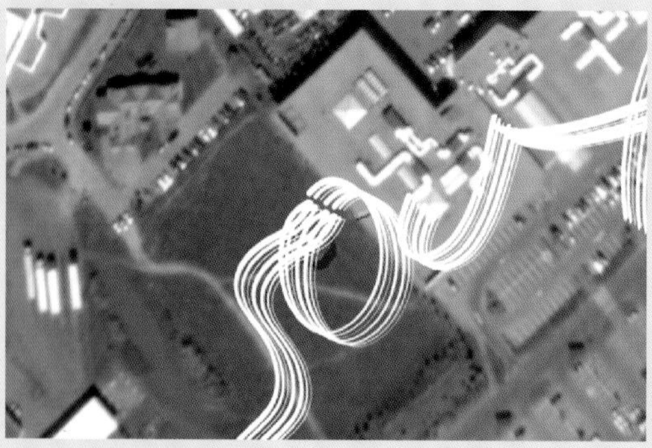

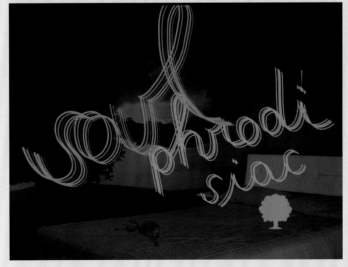

Design   Peter Anderson / Interfield Design
Project   Mayo
Category   TV title sequence
Date   2005

Created over a grid of translucent dark red squares, the
letters are cropped and fragmented like a puzzle. Small
graphic icons are also introduced into the grid.

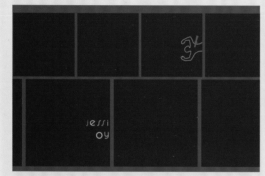

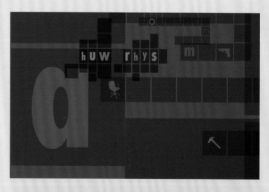

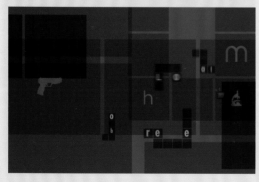

Design	Peter Anderson / Interfield Design
Project	Eroica / Bleak House
Category	TV title sequences
Date	2005

Two further title sequences from the same designer. These are more purely typographic in content. *Eroica* features an outlined serif font set in upper case: the outlines of the characters become fractured and animated in different line thicknesses. *Bleak House* relies on a crudely drawn ink-lettering style. The coarseness of the calligraphy is appropriate to the grim world of Dickens's story.

Design	Lewis Kyle White
Project	Type in Motion
Category	Self-initiated project
Date	2005

Fragments of typography become liquid in this self-initiated
project. What look to be typographic elements from
a signage system are stirred up into a liquefied state,
so that they seem suspended in space and to be turning
into paint or ink.

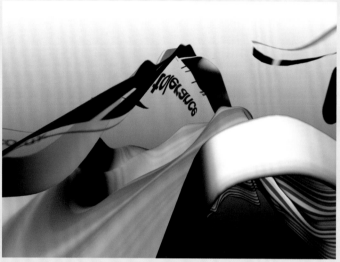

Design	Base Design
Project	BeTV
Category	Visual identity / TV ident
Date	2005

The project, an entire visual identity for a subscription-based television network in Belgium, includes the development of a corporate font which forms the basis of the logo and all other screen- and print-based graphics. The font has its roots in the American Typewriter font. However, the Be version has a softer, more curvaceous quality to it, with character finials ending in a larger, curved blob.

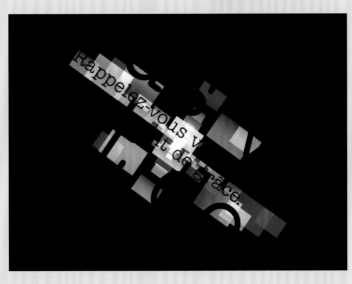

Design	Stiletto
Project	Viva Plus
Category	TV idents
Date	2002

This series of short idents created for the German music channel shows a stream of text-based information. The text feeds are cut and scrolled over a background mix of urban and natural-world images.

TEENS LISTEN TO AN ESTIMATED 10,500 HOURS OF ROCK MU BETWEEN THE SEVENTH AND TWELFTH GR. HOURS L

COLOGNE LOCAL TIME: 07:01, TUE 2002
SUNRISE: 08:54 SUNSET: 17:42

TIME:
07:01

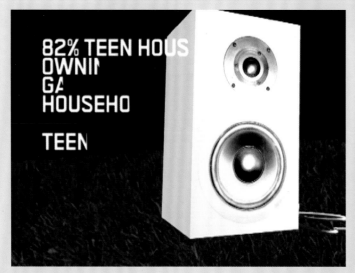

82% TEEN HOUS
OWNIN
GA
HOUSEHO

TEEN

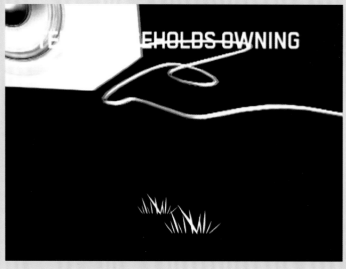

EHOLDS OWNING

OWNING IN-HOME VI
GAME SYSTEMS -
HOUSEHOLDS OWNING
DIGITAL CAME
TEEN HOUSEHOLDS O

YOUTH CULTURE- FAMILY : ARE CHILDREN TODAY MORE OR L
YEARS AGO ? BOX-MORE / 3X

HOROSCOPES. 55% DON'T.

YOUTH CULTURE- FAMILY : ARE CHILDREN TODAY MORE OR LESS SPOILED THAN CHILDREN 10 OR 15
YEARS AGO ? BOX-MORE / 3X LESS / 15% ABOUT THE SAME----------------------------ARE YOUR

GNE DA
Y 13:00
- 17 :00

COLOGN
E DAY
13:00 -
15 :00

N A CELL PHON
HONE

- 6%

WHAT DO KIDS 9 TO 12 LIKE TO EAT IN THE
MORNING:
42% CEREAL, 20% EGGS, 16% PANCAKES/WAFFLES, 6% TOAST

42%
CEREAL
20%
EGGS

Design	Studio for Virtual Typography
Project	ML
Category	Music video
Date	2004

This video was created for Loca Records in Brighton to
accompany music by ML. The text derives from
'Mittwochsgespräch', a poem by Helmut Heissenbüttel.
The typography is generated from a series of animated
circles that move around the screen to form the letters.
The circles also form concentric ripples in time to the music.

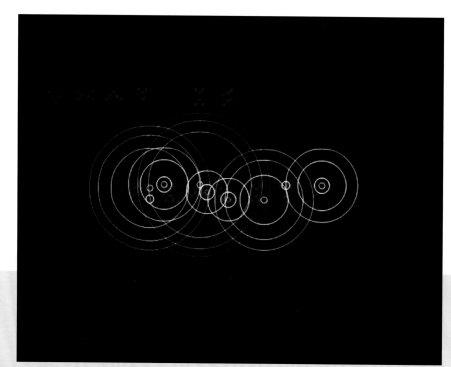

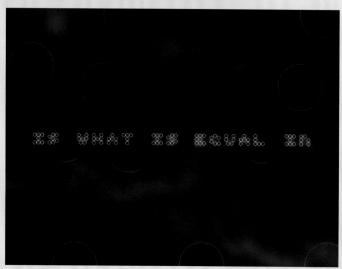

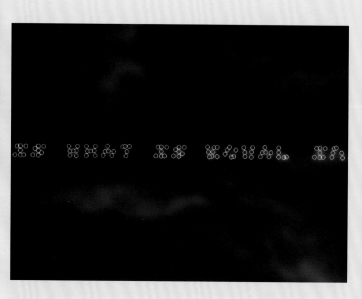

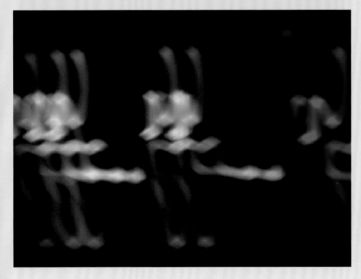

IS EQUAL EXPERIENCE EQUAL TO REALITY

Alignment
Describes the vertical edge of a column of type: for example, 'ranged left'.

Ampersand (&)
A short version of 'and', derived from the Latin ligature for 'et'.

Arabic figures
The most commonly used numeral system (1, 2, 3, 4, etc), based on traditional Arabic scripts. An alternative to roman numerals (I, II, III, IV, etc).

Ascender
The part of a lowercase letter that extends above the x-height, as in b, d, f, h, etc.

Bar
The horizontal stroke on characters such as A, H, e.

Baseline
The horizontal visual line on which all characters sit.

Bicapitalization
Uppercase letters used within compound words or phrases, also known as 'inter-caps'.

Body
In metal type, the rectangle of metal onto which the letter was cast. The term is also used in digital typesetting to refer to the notional space occupied by the letter.

Body type
The name given to a piece of text setting, usually set at a size below 14pt.

Bold
The description given to a thicker version of a typeface, also known as heavy or black.

Book
The name given to a weight of type similar to 'regular' but having a more solid structure and being fractionally heavier in weight. Designed to work well at body-text sizes.

Bowl
The rounded part of letters such as P and R and the upper part of the lowercase g.

Cap-line
The imaginary line that runs along the top of uppercase characters.

Centred
Alignment of a column of text in which each line of text is centrally aligned.

Counter
The enclosed negative space within a character.

Cursive
A flowing, script-like style of lettering.

Descender
The part of a lowercase letter that extends below the baseline, as in g, j, p, y, etc.

Dingbats
Non-alphabet-based characters, symbols or pictograms, also known as 'fleurons'.

Display type
Large and often decorative typefaces, traditionally used on posters to attract attention from a distance.

Drop cap
The first letter of a passage of text which is set in a larger point size than the rest of the body text.

Em
A unit of measurement derived from the width of the square body of the uppercase M.

Em-dash
A long horizontal dash, the width of an em.

En
A unit of measurement derived from half the width of an Em.

En-dash
A short horizontal dash, half the width of an Em.

Folios
The page numbers in a book or magazine.

Font
The contemporary term for 'fount', which refers to a single weight or style of a typeface.

Fount
The traditional term used for metal setting, which means a complete set of types comprising a proportionate number of each letter of the alphabet including all punctuation marks, etc.

Furniture
Pieces of wood or metal used in traditional letterpress setting to space type within a forme.

Geometric
A style of sans-serif font based on clean geometric shapes in which the o is a pure circle: e.g., Futura.

Gothic
An American term for sans serif. Also a term used to describe blackletter faces such as Old English and Fette Fraktur.

Grotesque (or Grotesk)
A term traditionally used to describe sans-serif typefaces: e.g., Akzidenz Grotesk.

Hot metal
The name used for traditional cast type setting.

Humanist
A style of roman type sometimes also referred to as 'Venetian': e.g., Gill Sans.

Italic
Type which echoes handwriting by having the letters slope up to the right; also known as cursive (kursiv).

Justified
A column of text which features characters aligning on both the left and right edges. Achieved by adjusting the amount of space between characters on each line of type.

Kern
In metal setting, the part of a letter that overhangs the main body of the character.

Kerning
The adjustment of the space between the characters.

Leading
In metal setting, thin strips of lead were inserted between lines of type to increase spacing. The term is still used in computer-based typography to refer to the distance from one baseline to the next.

Letterpress
A method of relief printing, usually using metal or wooden type characters.

Ligature
The connecting link between two letters that are joined together. The most common examples are fi and fl.

Light
A weight of type thinner than the conventional roman, regular or normal versions of a face.

Lining numerals
Figures that have the same height as uppercase characters.

Loop
The lower part of a lowercase g.

Lowercase
When all type was set by hand, two cases were used, one being arranged on a frame higher than the other. The upper case held the capitals, the lower case held the small letters (minuscules). See 'Uppercase' (below).

Majuscules
Capital or uppercase letters.

Minuscules
Lowercase letters.

Modern face
A kind of serif font (e.g., Bodoni) in which the point of maximum stress is central. The serifs of letters are at right angles to the vertical strokes and are of an even thickness, unlike in traditional serif fonts where they are tapered towards the end.

Monospace
Each letter is designed with the same width of body, so that a letter i occupies the same amount of space as an m. Predominantly used for tabulated setting.

Multiple Master
Typeface system introduced by Adobe in 1991 which allows the user to adjust the thickness and width of characters between pre-set parameters.

Non-lining figures
Figures with a non-standard height: e.g., the tail of the number 6 rises to the cap-height, with the bowl occupying the x-height, while the tail of a 9 descends below the baseline. Also known as 'old-style figures'.

Old face
Serif typefaces (e.g., Caslon) with an oblique stress, a gradual transition from thick to thin strokes in the curved letters and serifs tapered towards the end.

Point size
Refers to the visual size of the character: 1pt = 0.351mm (0.0138in). Traditionally typesizes were manufactured in 6pt increments: 6pt, 12pt, 18pt, up to 72pt, which is equivalent to 1 inch.

Ranged left
Alignment of a column of text, where all lines start at the same position on the left edge.

Ranged right
Alignment of a column of text, where all lines end at the same position on the right edge.

Recto
The right-hand page of an open book.

Roman
The name often applied to the Latin-based alphabet. It is also used to describe upright letters as opposed to sloping 'italic' letters.

Roman numerals
E.g., I = 1, II = 2, III = 3, IV = 4, V = 5, VI = 6, VII = 7, VIII = 8, IX = 9, X = 10, L = 50, C = 100, D = 500, M = 1000.

Sans serif
Typefaces without serifs: e.g., Helvetica.

Script type
A type style that imitates handwriting: e.g., Palace Script.

Serif
The projected finishing strokes at the ends of stems of letters. Thought to originate from stone-carved lettering, such as that on Trajan's Column in Rome, c. 114 AD.

Slab serif
Heavy rectangular serifs that may include a curved radius to the main stem, e.g., Clarendon, or square to the stem, e.g., Egyptian.

Small caps
Capital letters (majuscules) with a reduced height, similar to the height of lowercase letters (minuscules). Mainly used for setting acronyms and abbreviations.

Solid
Lines of type set without any leading are said to be 'set solid': e.g., 12pt type on 12pt leading.

Sorts
A term used in metal setting referring to individual bits of type as distinct from a complete font.

Stem
The main vertical or diagonal stroke of a letter.

Stochastic screen
An image generated using an apparently random spray of extremely small dots of colour, which allows very fine details to be reproduced. Also known as 'raster-screening'.

Terminal
A curve such as the tail of a cursive or script character; also known as a 'finial'.

Tracking
The adjustment of word and letter spaces applied to whole lines or passages of text.

Transitional
Serif typefaces that combine features of old face and modern styles: e.g., Baskerville.

Uppercase
When all type was set by hand, two cases were used, one being arranged on a frame higher than the other. The upper case held the capitals (majuscules), the lower case held the small letters. See 'Lowercase' (above).

Verso
The left-hand page of an open book.

X-height
The height of the main part of lowercase letters, also known as the 'mean-line'.